How to Hunt
Whitetail Deer

How to Hunt
Whitetail Deer

Luther A. Anderson

FUNK & WAGNALLS   NEW YORK

Library of Congress Catalog Card Number: 68–21717
Published by Funk & Wagnalls, *A Division of* Reader's Digest Books, Inc.

Printed in the United States of America
by American Book–Stratford Press, Inc.

Contents

How to Hunt Whitetail Deer

1
The Abundant Whitetail

WHEN THE AVERAGE HUNTER talks of big game he means, first and foremost, the three members of the American deer family—the whitetail, the mule deer, and the blacktail.

The whitetail, with which this book is concerned, is not only the most abundant big game animal in North America, but also one of the shrewdest. In the big game class only the bear is more skillful in dodging hunters and making himself difficult to bag. Eternal vigilance is necessary in order for this familiar and popular member of the deer family to survive, especially in the limited environment it prefers.

The hunter who can match wits with a woods-wise old buck—or even a young one—and win, will find that he has truly earned his trophy. The whitetail has shown remarkable ability in adjusting itself to the ways of man, increasing in numbers over the years even under the mounting pressure of modern hunting conditions. The whitetail is holding its own in the face of advancing civilization and even in populated areas with a minimum of shelter.

Evidently the whitetail is here to stay; a recent census shows more than 500,000 in the states of Michigan, Wisconsin, Pennsylvania, Minnesota, and Texas. A wide distribution is also noted for this species, extending from the Atlantic seaboard to the Pacific coast, and from Mexico in the south almost to Hudson Bay in the north.

Not many whitetails are found west of the Rocky Mountains, although a few inhabit the lower part of this range and the Columbia River drainage region. Some of the best states for whitetails—in addition to the five already mentioned—are Maine, New York, New Hampshire, Vermont, West Virginia, Arkansas, Arizona, Alabama, Florida, and Georgia. There is a total whitetail population in the United States of more than five million animals.

The white-tailed deer is noted not only for its shrewdness but also for its grace and fleetness. This deer is rhythm personified, crossing rugged terrain in smooth leaps and bounds. This swiftness of foot does not last long, for as soon as the animal reaches any sort of cover it begins to rely on evasive tactics rather than on speed to escape.

The whitetail, on the whole, is not a large creature; the

average mature whitetail buck runs about 200 pounds dressed, with a few of the better-fed and solitary bucks ranging from 250 to 300 pounds. These weights apply mostly to the northern deer: the whitetail of the north are usually about twice as heavy as those in the southern zones.

The Animal Itself

The whitetail derives its names from its conspicuous "flag," a rather long and broad tail measuring about fourteen inches in length. This tail has long brown hairs fringed with white above and is all white on the underside. The tail goes erect as the deer starts running and is waved slightly from side to side as long as the deer is in motion. It is usually a sign of a direct hit when the tail drops sharply and is kept that way.

As to body color, the whitetail is lighter than the western mule deer, its coat ranging from reddish brown to grayish tan. The summer coat is reddish in color, is worn for about three months, and is replaced usually in September by the winter coat. The summer coat is scanty, with little underfur, and is small protection against insects such as mosquitoes, blackflies, and gnats. This is often the reason the deer seeks the shielding and cooling waters of lake and stream.

In winter, the red summer suit is replaced by a thick pelage of grayish tan that is excellent camouflage in the dun cover at this time. In fall and winter, it is especially difficult to distinguish the deer from its surroundings.

The hair of the winter coat is about two inches long; the hairs are hollow, providing fine insulation from the cold, and the insulating qualities of the outer coat are further enhanced by an undercoat of soft, loosely curling hair next to the skin. With such insulation the deer can bed down in snow for long periods of time with no apparent discomfort and no thawing of the snow underneath.

In general, the whitetail, no matter where found, is whitish along the belly; has a white patch on the throat; a white band around the eyes; and white markings inside the ears and the inner side of each leg. The real trademark of this animal, however, is the sweeping tail, which is often a dead giveaway to the presence of the deer when it tries to flee.

The ears of the whitetail are smaller than those of the mule deer, and there is also a difference in the antlers. The main beams of the whitetail's antlers extend from the brow, curve backward slightly, and then curve out and forward in a flowing sweep. Spikes springing outward from the beams are rather evenly spaced and slightly forward of the vertical. The mule deer and blacktail have forked prongs on their antlers, which is not the case with the whitetail which has single prongs. The whitetail's antlers are solid, polished bone, reaching their peak size when the buck is eight years old. As he ages, the antlers decline in size, shape, and symmetry, becoming irregular and snaggy in appearance. In winter, of course, the antlers are shed, leaving the buck docile and shy. He is no longer the prize he was during the rutting season, when

he was swollen of neck and red-eyed, ready for a fight—
a splendid-looking animal throughout.

Like the mule deer and the blacktail, the whitetail is a
browser. He eats practically no grass, but subsists chiefly
on coarse-fibered plants and bushes, berries, fruits, nuts,
acorns, brush tips, twigs, shrubs, leaves, and certain
evergreens, notably cedar. The whitetail prefers cover
with many openings, and will haunt the fringes of the
deep woods rather than the heavier cover when not
overly molested. Unlike the mule deer, the whitetail is
not a migrating animal. However, it may change its range
slightly from time to time, especially in the winter when
it prefers to yard up in swamps for protection and food.

Increase in Population

Even in the face of great hunting pressure the whitetail
is increasing in numbers, a fact which endears it to game
experts and hunters alike.

Records also show that in the days of the Indian the
actual number of deer was probably less than it is today.
The size of the average animal was larger then, but the
deer herds did not flourish then as they do now. This is
due mainly to a change in forest conditions. At that time
large timber tracts prevailed, with few of the open areas
which deer prefer.

With the coming of the lumberman and the rancher
the heavy forests were gradually decimated, letting sunlight into much of the deer range, and stimulating the
growth of ground vegetation and young trees on which

deer feed. With an increased food supply the deer herds grew and flourished until they were plentiful and easily taken by anyone who wanted this game.

In the 1870's, both in the logging areas as well as in the agricultural belts, meat and hide hunters began depleting the herds. They did so to such an extent that by about 1900 the herds were at a low level. Restrictive hunting regulations were instituted in most of the deer states; and these, along with better law observance, resulted in the herds again growing to considerable size.

These laws, together with a steady regrowth of ground vegetation and saplings, gave the deer herds a big boost, with the result that now there are more deer in the United States than ever before. Naturally, the herds have had their ups and downs over the years, but now they seem to be pretty well established and on the increase.

An excellent example of how deer have increased in a given area can be noted in Pennsylvania. There were practically no deer in that state from 1905 to 1910. The chances for any kind of hunting season at any time seemed very remote. Sportsmen, especially, felt this way. Due to market hunting and forest fires which swept the land, the whitetail population had suffered a deep decline.

But something happened which changed the picture radically. The Pennsylvania Game Commission obtained 1,192 deer from game farms and other states and released the animals in various strategic counties throughout Penn's Woods. At about this time a statewide forest fire protection system was also instituted which helped save vegetation and trees and allowed thousands of acres of land to grow into brush and saplings, providing browse and cover that the whitetail needed greatly. Strict law enforcement measures were instituted to protect the does and end market hunting and illegal shooting. Within twenty years Pennsylvania had a deer herd which was estimated at a million animals; and today the number is still growing. The whitetail has come back in force in Pennsylvania and seems to be there to stay. This animal has a great reproductive capacity. Given half a chance, and with proper game management, it will thrive and furnish hunters with sport for years to come.

Importance of the Whitetail

That the whitetail is our most important game species is attested to in part by the annual army of deer hunters whose members take to the field at a goodly expense. Since earliest times deer have been known as objects of the chase, with their meat in much demand. In Europe, at one time the sport of deer chasing was largely enjoyed by the landed gentry and nobility, but in the United States today it is everyman's game. Hunting is a special American heritage; about twenty million people purchase hunting licenses each year.

The time when the deer was sought mainly for its food value and its hide is gone. Venison is very nutritious meat; the skin of the deer does make a very strong, soft leather, known as buckskin, and it is still being used for making leather jackets, gloves, and mitts; but the day of the market gunner and meat hunter is definitely past. Poachers exist, and always will exist, especially in the game areas; today, however, the average hunter is out mainly for the sport involved, rather than for the meat.

This sport plays a prominent part in the commerce of today, as it is especially important to many businessmen in the deer country who supply deer hunters with food, shelter, clothing, ammunition, firearms, guide service, gasoline, amusements, refreshments, and the like. There is a decided increase in activity in the major deer hunting areas when the hunters make their presence known during the deer season. A good many deer hunters, especially those from outside the local area, seem interested only in the pleasure they derive from the sport regardless of cost. Restaurants, hotels, clothing stores, outfitters, food shops, and taverns do a booming trade when the season is on.

It has been estimated that the cost of bagging a deer averages a little over a hundred dollars. This is definitely big business with so many hunters involved. Expenses are varied and many, especially when an out-of-state hunter, for example, goes for his deer. Traveling many miles, he not only must spend a good deal for gas and oil, but also for food and lodging en route. Then he encounters expenses during the time he is in the deer area. For example, he may spend the entire duration of his trip at some modern motel. And his non-resident license fee is quite high.

Even the local hunter will have to buy a license; equip himself with suitable clothing, gun, ammunition, and food; and perhaps put up in a camp, which he and his partners may have built at some expense. His gas bill may be staggering, especially if he is a "road hunter" or travels back and forth from home to hunting area many days during the season. But the true deer hunter is a dedicated soul who looks forward to the season and goes for his trophy regardless of the cost.

Fortunately, with laws being enacted and carried out as well as possible in the interest of conservation, the outlook for continued deer hunting is favorable. At the present time the deer population is probably as large as it has ever been; in fact, overpopulation problems arise from year to year which threaten the welfare of the deer. In this respect, the deer themselves are their own worst enemies.

Unlike most domestic animals, deer are immune to many diseases which might control their numbers. At the same time there is the matter of deer population versus food supply. In many areas the range is overgrazed; this is not so in the summer when food is plentiful, but occurs in the winter when the deer yard up and fail to find enough forage to keep them alive. As such starvation is harmful to all concerned, the conservation commissions have their hands full trying to balance the deer population with the food supply. One answer often resorted to, in certain areas, is the "any deer" law; that is, a deer of either sex may be shot.

It is the goal of the game experts to manage the deer herd in such a manner that the people will reap the greatest possible benefit over the longest period of time.

Laws and restrictions are therefore enacted to regulate the hunter's actions, not only for the good of the deer herd, but for the future of deer hunting in those areas.

Indiscriminate use of firearms, overbrowsing, forest fires, the shooting of deer of any size or sex, and violations of any sort are detrimental to the whitetail population. Such actions are also injurious to the hunters themselves, who must cooperate as a unit to keep the hunting secure for themselves and for future sportsmen. The future of whitetail hunting depends upon how the game is managed as well as how each hunter deports himself in the field.

The idea of conservation was perhaps uppermost in the thinking of Teddy Roosevelt when he said: "In hunting, the finding, and killing of game is after all but a part of the whole. The free, self-reliant, adventurous life with its rugged and stalwart democracy, the wild surroundings, the grand beauty of the scenery, the chance to study the ways and habits of woodland creatures—all these unite to give to the career of the wilderness hunter its peculiar charm."

2
Natural History

AN ANIMAL THE SIZE OF A WHITETAIL that has survived
the intensive hunting of the Indian, frontiersman, and
market gunner—not to mention the modern rifleman—
must possess uncommon sensitivities and faculties. This
is certainly true of the white-tailed deer. The senses of
scent, hearing, and vision, as well as an innate wariness,
have been developed to a high degree in the whitetail and
must be taken into full account when hunting.

Whitetails do make mistakes, and a man might
blunder right into an easy shot on occasion. It happens
every season, in fact. However, for real success with this
animal, the serious hunter must have an awareness of its
highly developed and nervous makeup to be a consistent

game-getter. He must know how it reacts to different situations, and determine both its strong and its weak points in order to make a showing during the hunting term.

Toward this goal, a study of the animal in its native habitat is recommended. Best results are obtained when the rifleman gets out into the field and unravels the daily life of this noteworthy animal. The more time he spends in this pursuit, before season, the better will be the results when he sets out with rifle in hand.

There is nothing more gratifying to many persons—the hunter, especially—than to happen onto a group of deer and watch how they conduct themselves in close proximity to man. The whitetail is a remarkable animal and knows how to survive and adapt itself to all conditions, particularly those encountered close to civilization. This is soon apparent by even a casual acquaintance with this woodland animal.

One thing the observant hunter will soon discover is that this animal is quite excitable and ready to take alarm at all times. In its native habitat it never lets down its guard. The whitetail has been persecuted for years, and its actions always show it. Starting with the day the deer is born it is forever in danger of its life. It must learn how to survive under adverse circumstances. This it does under the able tutelage of its mother, the doe. From her the whitetail fawn soon learns how to cope with natural predators such as the coyote, wolf, and bobcat, as well as other problems of survival.

Aside from its natural predators, the whitetail has to

contend with human enemies. Prime whitetail cover is easily accessible by car from nearby towns; the wilderness deer is no longer a remote animal and yet it survives. Its senses have been developed to a high degree to compensate for its environment and the predators with which it comes in contact.

The whitetail has an especially keen sense of smell which helps it to survive under adverse conditions. When alerted to danger the whitetail is quick to test the wind currents and find refuge in flight if the odors so indicate.

That is not to say that the deer will run from all strange and alarming odors; but it will certainly take note of them and become alerted. For example, during the summer season a deer will discover a man by scent (as well as hearing and vision), but it will not always run. Deer have become accustomed to humans from living so close to inhabited areas. During the summer months the deer are not molested to any extent. However, when the hunting season is on they become more suspicious of any predator, and are ready to head for safe quarters when danger is detected anywhere in the vicinity.

Along with a very keen nose, the whitetail has ears that are sharp and quick to pick up noises of any type. When there are sounds of an alarming nature the whitetail will warp its large ears in that direction and try to dissemble them. Then, along with its other senses, it will determine quickly whether it should move or not.

Some noises are indigenous to the cover, of course; others are foreign and disturbing. The whitetail must determine which is which; otherwise it would spend the day in headlong flight, for there are sounds emanating from the cover at all times.

The deer will not always flee. For instance, the sounds made by another deer are not alarming. But a predator has a different approach; and such sounds, along with scent and vision, will send the whitetail quickly into nearby cover.

The deer's vision is not as good as its other two senses, however. To begin with, deer are color-blind, and a human will appear to be just another part of the scenery when motionless and located upwind. A hunter can take advantage of the deer's limited vision, and approach to gun range if he moves only when the whitetail is looking the other way, and is quiet in his approach. Vision is one of the deer's weak points and this should be remembered.

The alert hunter takes cognizance of this weakness by keeping brush and foliage between him and the deer as much as possible, and advancing slowly and cautiously to within close shooting distance. In early times, when the Indian was after a deer in the more open country he would carry clumps of brush as a camouflage, hiding behind the bush and stealing ahead when the game's attention was directed elsewhere.

The whitetail is amazingly perceptive of movement, especially, and therein lies the rub in still-hunting and stalking. When game is sighted the hunter will have to be quick in mounting and sighting his rifle or the deer will be alerted immediately. In this respect, fast action is more alarming than slow, slight movement; but whatever the motion, the whitetail will be quick to detect it. Many years of persecution have resulted in the development of the deer's senses to a high degree, and to approach one close enough for a clean shot without detection is an achievement of the first water.

Let me point out that one type of motion might be alarming, and another might not. I have seen this demonstrated many times, especially when traveling through the deer woods in a car.

One instance is typical. One summer day I saw several deer just a short distance in the thicket. Stopping the car with the motor idling, I reached for my camera in the back seat, got out of the car on the side away from the deer, and then walked to the edge of the woods. No hasty approach. After the deer trotted away a bit, they stopped again. I moved in closer for more pictures before they retreated.

In contrast, I remember another occasion vividly, *during season,* when my partner and I sighted four deer alongside the road—a buck and three does. Excited at the prospect of a shot, my companion opened the car door on his side—toward the deer—and that was the last we saw of those four whitetails; even the does disappeared. No discreet withdrawal; they all turned tail.

Several times I have stalked deer in a canoe successfully and easily by keeping sound and motion to a minimum. For instance, there was the time on the Big Presque Isle River in northern Michigan when we saw a deer feeding on underwater plants. With three men in the canoe, I navigated the craft from the stern seat, sculling it very quietly.

We spotted the large deer some distance downstream.

Moving slowly and quietly when the whitetail had its head down, we managed to create an illusion of stability and approached to within 50 feet of the unsuspecting animal before it raised its antlered head and took fright. It made a whirlwind and water-splashing rush for shore.

Along with its sharp senses, the whitetail also excels in keeping alive and healthy by its ability to hide out and camouflage itself in most any part of its habitat. It is distinctly a "woods" animal. Always the whitetail will try to find range that is protective, never venturing far from cover during the daylight hours.

The whitetail has an uncanny ability to spend its time where the forest growth shields it; sometimes it is so thoroughly shielded that the hunter is unable to make a direct hit even when the deer is a short distance away.

As an illustration, one noon my partner and I returned to camp and were entirely unprepared for what we saw. A young buck was sauntering into the nearby second growth quite unconcernedly—until we showed up. My companion failed to see the deer immediately, but I had my rifle mounted and began firing straight at the deer.

Much to my dismay, the buck was in the thicket before I even raised my rifle. It kept on running, putting more trees and brush between us. I pumped five bullets into the immediate vicinity of that handsome buck but to no avail. The trees were thick and protecting, and the white-tail was smart enough to stay right in their midst.

"I didn't even see the deer after he started off," my partner confessed. "Too many trees and brush."

I did see the deer and I did get in some shooting; but

except for the target practice, it was a waste of time and ammunition.

In addition to its senses of smell, hearing, and vision, the whitetail is also a born skulker and hider. In much of the range an alerted whitetail can avoid hunters at will. A buck will prefer to hide out, rather than to make a run for it when hunters are present. Many a whitetail will just lie low and let the hunter pass; or detect the presence of the nimrod and keep out of sight and sound of the man approaching. This characteristic of lying low has been well developed, and is quite marked.

One trait that often works to the downfall of the whitetail is its sense of curiosity. However, this is not one to bank on. This inquisitiveness mostly results from the whitetail's inability to identify the person or animal at a distance because of its limited vision. In such an instance the whitetail may seem puzzled for a time; but when it does identify the object as a predator it will usually depart with speed.

Not all activity in the woods is going to frighten a whitetail, and this applies even to a watchful and wily buck. Deer like to see what is happening in their baili-wick, and will sometimes approach very close to the scene of action. This may happen when a crew is cutting timber or pulpwood in a deer area, or when hunters are cutting wood for their camp. To illustrate this type of curiosity I like to think of the time Ernie Bloomquist and I were cutting firewood for our hunting camp on the Hay Marsh Road in the Lake Superior–Mud Creek area.

We had burned a lot of fuel the first few days of deer

season and needed more shortly, so gathering an axe, a saw, and one rifle—my partner's—we started to work on a big birch deadfall back of camp. We carved off five heavy chunks of the giant tree and decided to take a rest. Wiping my brow, and putting the saw down, I looked toward the camp and there stood a large whitetail buck.

I remember telling Ernie to turn around slowly and reach for his rifle:

"There's a buck at the edge of the hemlocks near camp watching us. It's a long shot, but I think you can make it."

Moving very casually, Ernie picked up his carbine and shouldered it slowly. As the buck suddenly shook his head and started for cover, my partner squeezed off the shot and made a direct hit. Our actions were not exactly alarming, and that deer had satisfied its curiosity. A sudden noise will "spook" a deer, as will a sharp or loud noise; but the sounds and action emanating from routine woods work do not seem unduly disturbing to the neighborhood deer.

All in all, the whitetail is a remarkable and unique animal, and is one that offers a direct challenge to the hunter. Its defensive qualities have been developed to an amazing extent, for the whitetail really has seen some pretty drastic changes in its home conditions.

This deer has come to adapt itself to its environs, to human habitation, and most of all to seasons. One may see the deer at close range during the warmer months, not to mention during the winter season when the deer are yarding. At the same time this quarry makes itself very scarce when the foliage and protective cover of the forest is decimated in the fall, and the hunting season is in full swing. Now is the time to hide and skulk; and to take to the swamps and heavy thickets when molested. Instinct warns the deer to stay in the background as much as possible, and at this the whitetail is a past master.

Even nature works in the game's favor; in early October its reddish coat is replaced by a dull brownish-gray pelage. When the deer is attired in this garb the hunter must often look twice to be aware that a deer has appeared.

There are weak spots in the whitetail's defense system, however, and the hunter can take advantage of them. Not always will a deer detect danger; no deer is infallible and each is an individual. For success with this animal, the serious hunter can adapt himself to conditions and work out solutions. The more he learns about his quarry —how it lives, where and why, where it hides out at certain times of day, how it reacts at all times—the better are his chances of returning with a trophy when he pins a deer tag on his coat and heads for the woods.

3

Selecting the Deer Cartridge

WITH THE WEALTH OF BULLET SIZES available, the deer hunter has plenty of choice. One of the things he must first determine, however, is the type of action he wishes to use. Here he has his choice of bolt, slide, lever, or autoloader. The deer hunter will find one of these best to shoot and handle; and when he makes his selection, then he will decide on what cartridge he wants to shoot with it.

One of the favorites with the eastern hunter is the lever action, like the Winchester Model 94, the Savage 99-F, and the Marlin 336. Somehow this is the traditional deer hunting action because it looks like a deer rifle, and is rather fast. This is especially true in the newer models where the lever swings in a short arc.

20

The lever is easy to operate, but it works better for the right-handed hunter than for the man who shoots from the left shoulder. For the latter there is the pump action Remington 760A, the only deer rifle of its kind, and a reliable one. The Remington pump deer rifle makes a fine arm for the man who has used this action in his bird hunting just before the deer term; it is very fast—faster than the lever—and easy to sight along when putting in several shots on game.

The western hunter, on the other hand, will like the bolt action for its superb accuracy and its all-purpose capabilities. It is excellent on most varieties of game from rabbits to mountain sheep. To its credit, too, the bolt is the most foolproof of all actions. This is something the hunter in the western field really appreciates when he is far from civilization and a gun shop.

Then there is the autoloader, noted especially for its speed factor. Your shots come quickly when all you have to do is press the trigger and let the automatic action do the loading and ejecting. This is not the lightest rifle, however. For the eastern hunter, who may have to carry his rifle all day in the field, that is something to remember.

The deer hunter should select an action that handles nicely for him, and then the cartridge that suits the country he hunts in. Brushy areas are usually encountered when after eastern deer; and more open range when hunting the whitetail of the west.

Often the western hunter will want a sling, and will be shooting from the prone position. He will demand a rifle for long-distance shooting (such as one with a bolt action), and he will prefer high-velocity, sharp-nosed bullets that will carry long distances with a clean trajectory.

The woods hunter has other ideas. His shots will fall more in the 80- to 100-yard range, and they will be taken fast for the most part. A sling and a prone position will be out. His shots will be at the offhand and taken quickly. He will be shooting through brush much of the time, and at short range. This adds up to fast handling, and a rather light rifle pushing a heavy and blunt bullet. If that rifle has a flat trajectory, fine; but super-accuracy is not as necessary here as it is with the western rifle.

There are some rifles and cartridges that are just made for woods hunting. One of the perennial deer calibers is the lever action .30-30, time-honored and very popular where deer hunters gather. One of the best known is the Winchester Model 94, weighing 6¼ pounds, which is a solid frame hammer gun with 6-shot capacity, and a 20-inch barrel. This is the carbine model which is admired by many deer hunters, and it is a rifle that has accounted for more deer than any other.

Many a western hunter likes this caliber and rifle because it is light and handy and can be carried in the scabbard while hunting from horseback. Endless eastern hunters choose the .30-30 carbine, too; mainly, I'm sure they choose it because it is light, comparatively low in price, and adequate, in the hands of a fairly competent shooter, for white-tailed deer.

The .30-30 is not a long-range cartridge and never was intended to be; but it definitely is a "brush" cartridge and excellent in eastern whitetail cover. Since most whitetails are bagged at less than 100 yards, and since this cartridge has plenty of punch at that range for this quarry, the .30-30 continues to enjoy popularity in eastern deer district.

Ammunition for the .30-30 is available throughout the country. It is almost as commonplace in sporting goods stores as the popular .22 caliber.

The deer hunter is an individualist, however, and many hunters will want a caliber in the big-game category such as .30-06, .270, .300, .303, .308, and .300 H & H Magnum seen often in eastern whitetail cover. Among these calibers the .300 and the .30-06 are high on the list with many "brush" hunters, even though these are more powerful than required in bagging the whitetail.

It is a fact that a cartridge of superlative power is much better than one which is deficient and light; and in this respect anything less than the .250 is just that, and is prohibited in many states. You can kill a deer with a .22 Hornet or a .218 Bee, but it is more likely that you will just wound it with this intermediate caliber. A few inches from a vital spot and the game will escape in a wounded condition.

Following is a list of effective deer calibers.

The *.30-30* is powerful enough and is an efficient cartridge when the bullet is well placed.

The *.250-3000* has a flatter trajectory than the .30-30 and is good where the country is not too brushy.

The *.250 Savage* is a light deer load, excellent

for the expert shot. However it is no longer being made.

The *.257 Roberts* is a bit more powerful than the .250-3000 and a proved deer caliber cartridge.

The *.270 Winchester* is good for the more open country. It is a fine, flat-shooting cartridge and powerful enough for big-game hunting.

The *.300 Savage* is a classic among deer loads. It has a caliber and action ideal for deer hunting in brush, as well as on the more open range for deer, moose, bear, elk, and antelope.

The *.30 Remington, .32 Winchester Special, .32 Remington,* and *.303 Savage* cartridges are similar to the .30-30 and are potent on whitetail deer.

The *.35 Remington* is adapted to the Remington Autoloading Rifle and Remington Slide Action, and excellent in woods hunting for whitetails. It has brush-penetrating ability plus.

The *.243 Winchester* and the *6 mm.* are also fine deer cartridges.

There is a trend nowadays toward the lighter calibers, such as the .243 Winchester and the 6 mm., in some of the whitetail range, and for good reason: These rifles are easy to carry, have high velocity, and kill by shock. In whitetail country such as the northern Mexican Sonora and parts of Texas where the range is open, many of the shots are long. With their flat bullet trajectory these cartridges carry long distances and have sufficient sectional density for good killing power. The added length of this cartridge results in surer kills and better accuracy.

Both the .243 and 6 mm. are lightweight rifles. They are smooth handling, and excellent at ranges of 200 yards or so. Definitely, however, they are not "brush" cartridges, but are meant for hunters who seek the white-tail where the trees and cover is only scant.

Definitely, too, vermin loads are not for deer. They can be used, but they are crippling rather than killing.

The cartridge for woods deer must be heavy and blunt, not deflected by brush. The 180-grain .300 Savage is certainly one of these; so is the .35 Remington, not to mention the ever-popular .30-30 and .32 special calibers.

The bigger calibers like the .30-06 and .308 will buck brush, and put the deer down for good when the hit is at all in the vitals. Nothing is more frustrating than to see your deer go down for a moment and then take off as though nothing had happened, to vanish completely because of the inadequacy of the cartridge. Lean to the heavier calibers for sure killing power. Although you may find yourself a bit tired from toting a rather heavy firearm you will know you have an adequate deer gun.

Choice of cartridge, as well as action, is a matter of personal taste. Take your pick in the deer gun and cartridge, and make the best of your option.

You can use a shotgun for deer, as well. When shooting rifled slugs or buckshot with this arm you will get excellent brush penetration. With the use of good sights, such as a low-power scope, you will effect quite accurate shooting.

Buckshot in the No. 0 is effective to about 35 yards, and No. 00 makes good contact at 50 yards. Rifled slugs are almost rifle-like in accuracy and deadly to about 75 yards.

One of the best shotguns for deer is the full choke 12-gauge shooting rifled slugs. Buckshot is killing in this gauge, as well. This shot has the advantage over slugs in populous areas because the pellets quickly lose their energy and do not travel far. A full choke 12-gauge with Magnum loads will pattern half of its shot within a 30-inch circle at 50 yards. It is fully effective on deer, especially if the shot reaches the vitals, such as the heart-lung area or the neck. Test your shotgun in the field before using it as a deer gun.

One advantage in using the shotgun for deer is your familiarity with the gun, providing you have done some small game hunting prior to deer hunting. When he is familiar with the action, the deer-getter will be on the game quickly, and that is half the battle in whitetail hunting.

Rifled slugs can also be used in the 16 and 20 gauges, and the .410 caliber. The 20 and .410 are too light for this quarry, however, and should never be used on deer. The 12-gauge is really reliable, with the rifled slug leaving the muzzle with a velocity of 1,600 feet per second, and having 2,400 foot-pounds of energy. Best results are obtained with the special models designed for slug shooting. These include the Ithaca Model 37 Deerslayer, and the Remington Model 870 Brushmaster. Equipped with a receiver peep sight, such as the Williams, or a low-power scope such as a 2½X, these guns are very potent on deer; and in the 20-inch or 22-inch barrel they are very fast handling, considering their size.

4
Rifle Sights and Sighting

NO RIFLE IS BETTER THAN ITS SIGHTS. If you can't get a clean and accurate sight picture, you won't hit. Let's take a look at the open sight that fits in pretty well and is good enough on close shots.

The open sight may be all you need in your brand of deer hunting, especially in brushy cover. Some successful deer hunters use no other. With the open sight they bag their deer times without number, and it is very popular with "brush" hunters. The best open sight to use is the wide "U" or "V" such as found on the Savage 99 carbine, or a shallow U with a white line marking the center. These are easy to see through and line up the game accurately.

The man using the open sight is apt to overshoot. This

tendency is partially overcome with the shallow open sight, but not entirely. The one to avoid in this respect is the high buckhorn sight which cuts off much of the field of view.

One objection to the open sight is that it is fairly adequate on close shots but deficient at ranges of 150 yards or more. This is a weakness in the sight which should not be overlooked by the hunter who does hunt deer at long ranges.

You can get by with the open sight. It is traditional with the deer hunter, but it is being replaced by the peep and the scope sight—the latter especially. Time was when you were regarded as an eccentric if you showed up at the deer camp with a scope sight. Not today. With deer rifles being stepped up in caliber and class, more and more rifles are coming equipped with the higher-quality sights.

The next degree up from the open sight is the peep (aperture sight). The deer hunter usually will have this sight installed on the rifle by some gunsmith and it will set him back a few dollars. But there is consolation that he will be the better for it since no open sight allows as much view of the game as the peep. Leading, especially, is easier with the peep in that you can see both under and over the game, and line up the sights on the target accurately. The peep is also better for the man with rather poor vision. Instead of looking *at* it, as in the open sight, the shooter looks *through* it.

With the open sight, the eye must focus on three things at the same time: the rear sight, the front sight, and the target. With the peep sight the shooter has only to look at the front sight and the target, while the eye automatically centers the game in the aperture.

The peep sight is quicker and more accurate than the open sight on running game in thick cover. The game can be seen clearly through the peep at all times, and the shooter can draw down on the game more accurately than he can with the open sight.

All this, however, hinges on using a peep sight that has a large opening. Most peep sights come equipped with small discs screwed in the aperture. These should be removed for deer hunting so the shooter can use the large opening instead. With this generous aperture he will have a wide field of view and be able to pick up the game clearly and quickly. The wide aperture is easy to use, especially if it is coupled with a clear front sight such as the ivory or red bead. Red is preferred for its stand-out qualities.

Some of the disadvantages of the peep sight are that the aperture will fill with snow or rain, and that it is somewhat deficient in poor light. But the wide aperture can be kept clean easily, and it can be seen through even in shadowy woods, so those objections are overruled. It is fast enough, and it is accurate up to 100 yards, and it is easy to use. It is a good sight both for standing and moving game.

The Lyman Cocking Sight is one of the best. It is fixed so that it jumps away when the trigger is pulled, and will not strike the eye.

At the head of the list we have the scope sight. It is the

latest improvement in sights. A flat-shooting deer rifle equipped with a quality scope will afford excellent shooting. It is accurate to a hair-splitting degree, and at some distance. The distance angle is not so important in eastern whitetail hunting, but accuracy is.

The scope sight is also exceptional because it is a boon to the man with failing eyesight. The scope is superlative for early morning and evening hunting also, for it has light-gathering power. For game identification it is really worthwhile, especially when the hunter is unable to distinguish with the naked eye whether the deer is a buck or doe. The scope is not as fast for running shots as the open and peep sights, but this disadvantage is offset by its other qualities, notably its accuracy and clarity on the target.

This is where the lower power, such as the 2½X, enters the picture. The low-power scope sight is exceptional for the close-range snap shot so common in the eastern field. Not only does the low-power scope offer light-gathering capabilities, but it gives the shooter a wide field of view. That is something to consider.

One must avoid the high-power scopes for deer. These scopes suffer from vibrations caused by unsteady holding. As the power of a scope is stepped up the vibration is increased. Nothing over a 4X should be used for deer hunting, and the latter power should be used only where the cover is rather sparse and open.

A good scope, like the 2½X or 3X, helps the shooter to aim, to see the game clearly, and to discern the spot he is fixed on at the time he takes the shot. The scope will not increase the accuracy of the rifle or flatten the trajectory, but it will render the target clearer, larger, and easier to hit.

Once the rifleman uses the scope and gets the hang of it, he will never go back to the iron sights. With the scope, the sighting is clear and everything is on the same plane. Using the scope often makes the difference between a hit and a miss.

It must be pointed out, however, that the scope sight does have disadvantages. Where the range is very close the scope sight is practically useless. The target becomes a blur, filling the scope completely and preventing accurate aiming. When rain or snow is the prospect the scope is not so good, either, for the scope magnifies the particles of moisture.

In heavy cover the trees viewed in the scope sight will distract the aim of the hunter to some extent. In this case the open and the peep sights are better.

The answer to all these objections is the combination of *both* iron and scope sights. For all-around work the scope should be mounted so that iron sights can be used if necessary. Equipped with swing-away scope mounts, the iron sights can be left intact, and can be used where the scope is inoperative. In fact, should the hunter wish it, with the proper mounting, he could remove the scope sight entirely and use the iron sights.

These occasions occur only rarely, however, even in brush hunting, and the scope sight takes first place in the deer hunting field. With this sight the hunter will be able to make more clean kills, and score more consistently all-around than he would with either the open or the peep sights. The scope should be strongly and solidly made, and the mounts carefully engineered. Most of today's scopes do meet these specifications.

They must be accompanied by the proper reticules, too; the best are the crosshairs, post and dot. For most brush hunting, the post and the dot take preference. The post must be large and sharp enough to stand out clearly, and the dot should also be large enough so that the shooter can pick it out quickly on the running shot. The crosshairs are at their best when the shot is at long range and taken with deliberation. This is something that does not happen too often in brush hunting.

The deer rifle should be sighted in at the 50-yard range and from the prone position. Shoot a slow group of 7 or 8 shots at the target with the type of ammunition you intend to use in hunting. Study the group and determine how the rifle is shooting, and if the sights need adjusting *move the rear sight in the direction you want the hits to go, both for elevation and windage.*

For instance, if you shoot a group and find that its center is to the right of the bulls-eye, you must move the rear sight to the right to correct. If you're shooting high, move the sight up. These adjustments are simple enough with the open sights, where the rear sight is moved in its notches, but a bit more difficult with the aperture sight, where the adjustments are made in minutes of angle and with a micrometer. The aperture sight and the scope sight are best adjusted by a gunsmith.

Keep adjusting the sights, if necessary, until you have

the rifle zeroed-in to shoot a close group. On-the-dot accuracy with the deer rifle is not exactly necessary; but get it as close and precise as you can, and chances are that you will do all right in this department. Proper sights and sighting are all-important in bringing the game to bag.

5

The Rifle
on Moving Deer

THE PECULIAR MOTION of the whitetail deer must first of all be taken into account by the rifleman who wishes to down it. Compared to the antelope, which bounds away with an even gait, the whitetail is a broken runner. It speeds through the brush with long and short leaps, skimming over logs, deadfalls, and knolls, providing a difficult target for anyone to catch through the sights of a rifle.

When startled, the whitetail goes away at a fast and uneven clip. In such a case the rifleman must make his play before the deer gets out of sight, and this calls for none other than the snap shot, quick and smooth if at all possible. Even when the deer is motionless the shot must be taken with dispatch, for at any time it may start moving, and the shot rendered much more difficult.

I hardly recall anything but a moving shot at a deer. It is a characteristic of the whitetail that it is always on the go. When the hunter is hiking through the woods his shots will usually be on game that is alerted and traveling.

I recall one shot that looked easy because the deer was close, but proved to be quite difficult. I caught sight of the whitetail just as it saw me. Early in the morning the deer was already bedded down, but on a small incline. Gravity was in its favor. It looked as if I had the buck in a pocket, however. The deer went away with a rush. With rifle raised and following for a lead I waited until he had finished his first wild dash. As he reached a small clearing I managed to line up the sights. I fired and missed as the buck went behind a screen of balsam; but following his leaps I managed to hold the rifle just a bit ahead of him and pressed the trigger again just as the deer went over a log.

Right at the top of his bound I could almost feel that the shot connected. I was right. The buck went down and I had my deer for the season.

The bouncing motion of a running whitetail renders it a very difficult target. When the motion of the whitetail is analyzed, however, it will be found there are two positions when the shot is stable: when the deer is at the top of its bound, and when the animal touches the ground.

At these two times the whitetail is reversing movement, like a coin thrown in the air. At the top of the bound and when it reaches the gound, motion is at a minimum; so if the shot is taken at either of these two positions the rifleman has a stationary target.

Naturally, he will have to lead. That lead will depend on the speed of the animal, the angle, the hunter's reaction time, and the distance. In this regard, it always pays to take a chance and shoot. Instinctively the deer will try to bluff you out of a shot by its noisy escape, but this tactic should be completely disregarded.

To the novice, the running deer will be altogether a chancy target to be taken only by luck. This is especially true because of the spectacular retreat of the deer. The initial racket, as well as the speedy retreat, often is enough to throw a man into a dither. The uproar is all out of proportion when the startled whitetail bursts out of its hiding place.

This type of shot is definitely typical of deer hunting. Only recently it happened to a young hunting friend of mine as we were just turning off the main trail to hunt a small slashing. My comrade was slightly ahead of me at the time. As we were climbing a small ridge, a buck leaped up with a snort, and fled with snow literally flying from its hoofs as it went downhill.

Not expecting to see deer this early in the hunt, my companion was entirely unprepared and carrying his rifle over his shoulder. The veteran hunter might have steeled himself to this encounter, but not my partner. Somehow he mounted his rifle. In a quick, desperate struggle with himself, he lined the sights on the departing tail of the buck, and got off two quick shots. They were both misses.

The speeding whitetail soon gained the shelter of the heavy brush, and my young comrade, none too acquainted with the moving target, lowered his rifle and shook his head in disgust. He fared better later on in the season, however, and did manage to bag his deer—on a running shot.

Surprises are the order of the day where deer are concerned. To prepare himself for these emergencies, the skilled deer hunter always carries his rifle in a fast-mounting position. First of all he must make sure that his rifle is right for him and handles well. When in the field he should carry it so that it comes to shoulder easily.

There are differences of opinion about the best carrying position, but after much experimenting I have found that cradling the rifle under the right arm, with the muzzle pointing at the ground, is fast, safe, and comfortable. The left hand quickly slides to the fore-end, the right hand to the trigger, and the rifle is mounted in one sweep. There is no lost motion. It is an easy carry.

To some hunters, like my young companion after his encounter with the buck, the shooting of moving deer appears to be something bordering on the miraculous. To the rank amateur who has never tried his hand at anything but stationary objects, it might appear so. But to hit a moving deer, and a rapidly disappearing one to boot, can be done and often after just one season of practice.

Pre-season training, both on the rifle range and in the small-game field, is the answer. And that is training of the right sort, always with the necessity of making a quick and sure shot in mind: the snap shot, no less. The deer hunter must master the mechanics of holding, aiming, trigger squeeze, and calling his shot, and go on from there.

For the running deer can be hit, and there is this in the deer hunter's favor: if he can become a quick, cool shot on the rifle range, he should be able to bag his deer time and time again, both standing and moving. The deer-getter need not be the best marksman in the world. That is, he need not hit the bulls-eye nine times out of ten at 100 yards. But he must be able to shoot rapidly, taking the deer when it is at its best position for a shot, and with the right lead.

He wants confidence in himself. When a man is able to shoot well in a properly relaxed manner, both in slow- and rapid-fire, he will make a good shot in the game field. He must shoot with care, always with a quick and shifting target in mind so that he has his rifle on the quarry in short order.

That is deer hunting.

And that points to timing. The rifleman must effect a good shooting position and balance himself. When the game breaks for cover he must bring the rifle up on the same plane as the quarry and take the shot as quickly as he is able, or the deer is gone. He must act not haphazardly, but with accuracy.

All the while he must keep his eyes on the target. He should have so much training in the mechanics of rifle shooting that the mounting, firing, and ejecting is done automatically.

Bullet Placement

On the running target you still will have to try to strike a vital spot, and one of the best is the heart-lung area. Other vital spots are the head, the neck, and the spine. The latter three are entirely possible when the deer is stationary, and especially when facing you head on, but this type of shot is hard to get.

The veteran hunter on a stand might try for the neck, brain, and spine, but from my observations he will be lucky to find a deer that will stand long enough for such a shot. Certainly a shot in either of these places will kill a deer with a minimum of meat spoilage, but they are chancy at best.

The heart-lung area offers a better place to place your bullet, especially on the running shot. When aiming for the heart the hunter must realize that it is behind the left shoulder and relatively low. Add to this the fact that the deer itself is not a tall animal. The hunter may find himself shooting through brush or tall grass to hit the animal in this area. A shot in the heart-lung area is usually fatal, however, and a well-placed bullet from an adequate deer rifle will usually drop the deer right in its tracks.

A paunch shot must be avoided, if at all possible. There is a possibility that it will stop the deer somewhat, but more than likely the shot will be only a crippling one. The animal may still travel for miles. Should the hunter recover the animal after a paunch shot he will find that the meat has acquired a bad taste. In fact, the sooner he can recover a wounded animal, the better.

When the deer presents a straightaway running shot the bullet can be placed in the anal region and drive fatally into the spine or chest. This type of shot happens frequently, especially when the deer is running.

Wounded Deer

A well-placed bullet simplifies everything. Every precaution should be used to strike the deer in the vitals and drop it then and there. As this is not always possible, and the deer fails to fall within sight of the hunter, it is incumbent upon him to follow up the shot, usually at once.

Many times a deer will continue to run smoothly even after taking a direct hit. It may speed along until it reaches heavy cover, and then begin to show signs of distress. After suffering a mortal wound more than one deer has run out of sight before dropping. This points definitely to examination of the trail after a shot even if the deer simply has vanished. With snow on the ground the trail will be easy to follow. But even without this factor it pays to head in after the animal and look for patches of hair which may have been shot off, or splashes of blood where the deer has traveled.

Often the hunter can tell immediately if the deer has suffered a hit. Most often the animal will betray its condition in a change of pace. If the deer is running and speeds up when the shot is fired, there is every possibility that the bullet has made contact.

But a fatal shot will not always drop it then and there. A whitetail has tremendous vitality and energy for its size. It may accelerate its pace, or slow down upon being wounded. Whatever the reaction, trailing is indicated. If the wound is vital you may find the deer in the first patch of brush that it has entered. However, you may have much farther to go.

There was a time when the hunter was cautioned to wait an hour or so for the deer to lie down and stiffen up. This procedure might be satisfactory in a little-hunted area, but in those places where many other nimrods are patrolling the cover it is far better to head in on the trail at once.

Examine every clump of cover very carefully along the trail, and be prepared for any sudden appearance of the animal. This process of trailing a wounded deer is identical with that of trailing one in good shape. The deer will expect to be followed, and even when badly wounded will always be watching its backtrail.

Look for signs of blood, mostly. But there are other indications of a wounded deer, usually a wavering and uncertain trail. Do your best to follow up the animal. You may find it just around the next bend, or you may not find it at all, but either way you will have the satisfaction of knowing for sure whether you hit the deer or not, and where you hit it.

6
Essential Equipment

THERE'S MORE TO DEER HUNTING EQUIPMENT than rifle and shells, and one of the more obvious and important items is clothing. There are other incidentals like binoculars, compass, knife, pack sack, sleeping bag, etc. I have seen some hunters cut their hunting day short because of improper clothing, such as ill-fitting boots or a poorly selected coat.

Clothing *is* important. The idea is to dress comfortably without bulk, and this is entirely possible in modern day garb. Select outer garments with a soft finish to avoid scraping noises when moving through brush, and here I point definitely to wool, as old as the hills and about as durable.

Let's start with the coat. The one I consider perfect for deer hunting is the woolen mackinaw, bright red or orange, soft-textured, and generous in cut. Whether you choose buttons or zippers makes little difference, but the material must be virgin wool.

If you're hunting in Texas you're better off with an insulated jacket, but the deer hunter in the northern tier of states will want warm, serviceable clothing to prepare himself for cold weather, which is the rule rather than the exception.

Trousers and breeches should be sturdy wool as well. One of the best in trousers for the deer hunter is the 100% virgin wool Malone pants. These are amazingly tough and durable. Two separate yarns are spun and twisted together in weaving this fabric. Malone is the only factory which makes this type of fabric, and it's one of the specialties of Eddie Bauer, outfitter, of Seattle, Washington. Malone fabric is very sturdy, provides real protection from the cold, has strength to resist tearing by briars and brush, and is snow and rain repellent.

Wear two shirts—one a lightweight sports shirt of gabardine and the other a top shirt of virgin wool on the order of a Pendleton or Woolrich. Above this wear a scarlet goose-down insulated vest, with a zipper front and two large pockets lined to serve as hand warmers for wintry days. When the weather turns warm the hunter can well discard his hunting coat and get along nicely with the insulated jacket.

In underwear, the two-piece, part-wool type is recommended for the deer hunter in the colder states. For the man who must be out in sometimes near-zero weather, and does his hunting from a stand, the two-piece thermal underwear is a boon and a blessing. Dressed adequately, the hunter can take freezing temperatures.

The same hunter will want woolen socks, without a doubt; one pair of nylon next the skin, let's say, and one or two pair over that of wool, worn in rubber boots. Wool not only keeps the feet warm, but cushions them. Used with an inner-liner, woolen socks worn in adequate footgear will go far toward making the hunt a success.

The boots must be large enough to accommodate two pairs of woolen socks. They must be comfortable, warm, and waterproof. Don't settle for leather footgear in the snow country. Insulated rubber boots are top notch; for all-around comfort, however, I go for the Maine-type boot, with rubber bottoms and leather tops, which are no more than 8 or 10 inches in height.

Get the best in footgear. You're on your feet much of the time, and your feet have to feel warm and well cushioned or you're in trouble.

A cap with earflaps in a bright orange is a must. You have a choice of leather, fur, or wool, or a combination. Try on a couple for size and feel. But stress the safety angle. A bright red or orange cap, with accent on the orange, stands out sharply in the deer woods and marks you definitely as a human, not a deer. If you wear a brilliant red or orange jacket your presence in the deer woods is readily apparent to any deer hunter, except the most color-blind, and let's hope this hunter is the rare exception!

I wear woolen gloves, red in color, for the colder days.

At one time I wore woolen mitts, but they are a hindrance. You can purchase regular shooting mitts with a trigger finger for either right or left hand. Another good idea for a hand covering is a glove with a woolen back and a leather palm. Many deer hunters get along very well without gloves, warming their hands when necessary by placing them in their pockets.

A sharp hunting knife carried in a sheath is needed to dress the kill. If you don't like the idea of the longer knife there is no reason that the pocket knife with a four-inch blade, if nicely sharp, will not suffice. When cleaning a deer you will get your hands bloody no matter how long the blade. The pocket knife has the advantage of taking up little room and never being in the way like the sheath knife.

Always carry a watch. You'll consult it many times during the day for one reason or another, and it certainly will be an aid in keeping appointments, both before the hunt as well as during the hunting day.

In eastern cover I find very few whitetail hunters using a sling on their rifles as an aid in shooting. There may be some open spaces like the fire burns in Pennsylvania and Michigan where a long shot is in order, and where the sling will come in handy as a rifle-steadying device, but these times are few and far between.

An ordinary carrying sling is a different matter, and is preferred by many deer hunters for carrying the rifle over the shoulder easily either when returning from the hunt or when dragging out a deer. It should not be listed as an "essential," however.

Carry a short length of heavy rope against that magic

time when you drag out your deer. You may want to keep this in your car or camp, however, instead of on your person, unless it is very short and you keep it in your coat pocket. You can drag out your buck by the antlers, but a piece of rope tied to this appendage offers a better grip for two or more hunters.

One item which takes up very little space and is worth its weight in gold on many occasions is the compass. Get one that is easy to read, like the Marble's, with an arrow pointing to the north, so there is never any doubt as to its positive end. One handy compass is the kind which pins on your coat lapel and is quick and easy to read. Another type which you might prefer is the compass with a hinged cover to protect the glass face, about the size of a pocket watch. This one can be kept in your upper left hand coat pocket, and secured with a cord.

Another item to top off the essential equipment to carry with you is a field glass or binoculars. There are occasions when your scope sight will help you look over and identify a certain object, but the rifle scope is not nearly as efficient as a good glass. For one thing this instrument will help you when combing a poorly lighted piece of cover for game. A quality binocular in a 6x30 or 7x35 is a good choice for eastern cover. Select the lower power rather than the higher because the former offers more field of view. This is important when studying the area extensively.

One of the biggest problems the deer hunter is faced with is finding the quarry, and a binocular is a specific help in this job of deer-detection. A good glass will also pick up light and afford a much clearer picture than the naked eye. The eastern whitetail hunter especially needs a glass to help him probe something as hard to spot as the camouflaged deer.

He should keep it on the light side, however, so that it will not hinder his movements. This goes for the outfit as a whole, also. Avoid bulky garments and equipment. In this day of insulated garments and specialized outdoor gear the deer hunter can travel light and with real comfort.

A pack sack is usually a must, and the Duluth-type pack is one of the best for the deer hunter. It is the regulation lumberjack pack, waterproof, easily carried, and capable of holding a wealth of gear and grub in good style.

Another piece of equipment you may want whether staying in a tent or a board camp is a sleeping bag. One of the best is the 100% goose down, the "go light" choice of backpackers, outdoorsmen, and especially deer hunters. A quality bag, like the Eddie Bauer Kara Koram, has a comfort range of zero to 65°. That's just what the doctor ordered for comfort in the deer camp. With the addition of an air mattress and a good tent, like the outside frame umbrella tent, you can set up camp almost anywhere in the deer range, and be right there at all times for the hunting, morning, noon, and night.

There is a lot to be said for instant hunting, and your chances of bringing home venison are so much better when you're there in deer cover throughout season, and when you're all set for the weather.

7
Hunting
from a Stand

ONE OF THE MOST SUCCESSFUL ways to hunt the whitetail
is by waiting for them at a stand. Some of the old timers
call it trail-watching, or "posting." In this method the
hunter lets the deer come to him, rather than carrying the
action to the quarry. When he plays the game expertly he
has a chance of securing better shots.

What the whitetail hunter does in this procedure is to
find a partially concealed spot on a promising runway,
and then wait quietly and patiently until the deer walks
within gun range.

Whitetails are like humans in the respect that they
follow the paths of least resistance, traveling the trails
they are accustomed to using during the summer. These

trails are well-established and strategic runs that take them from their bedding grounds to their night grounds, and vice versa. The deer are moving; the hunter is motionless. Result? The game will usually approach the posting area unaware of the rifleman's presence, and the latter will be able to get a shot at either a standing target or one that is just moving slowly.

And let me point out that when many hunters are roaming about, such as during the first of season, this type of hunting is especially effective. The man watching at an advantageous stand has things in his favor. He is in an excellent position to bring home a trophy, perhaps one of the bigger bucks.

However, deer runs may shift with the seasons, so that it behooves the hunter to determine which runs the game are using now when deer season is on, not during the summer. They may be using the same runs, but you will never know until you make a survey just prior to opening day. You may even have to change your stand during the season, too, for the deer may leave a spot which is too often hunted.

Trail-watching is a man's game. It is a tough one, but it is one that pays off in the long run. You may tramp all day and see nothing but tails, especially when the ground is dry and noisy. The game has the edge on you. With their keen senses deer can locate you first. But when you find a well-used deer run and stay there, you will have the advantage.

The best time to hunt at a stand is from daybreak to 9 A.M. when the deer are moving out from their night grounds, and from 3 P.M. until dusk when the game is moving back to its night range. Of these two periods the early morning hours are best. The deer have not been molested by hunters during the evening and are moving to their daytime beds. At this time they are not too frightened. They are always alert and watchful, of course, but not alarmed.

I once saw a buck returning to his night cover literally skimming over the logging road he had to cross in the process. He'd been hunted all day, no doubt, and was prepared for the worst. He wasn't just walking, as the game usually is early in the morning; he was traveling like the wind, scared as a cat, with his paunch close to the ground.

On the first three days of season, especially, the trail watcher stands a fine chance of a shot. Just sit there. Men are moving. Take the case of deer-hunting centers like Ironwood, Michigan, or Hayward, Wisconsin, the first day of season. There's a world of activity; the red-coated army has moved in, and every camp, hotel and motel is filled to overflowing by the night before season. The hunters will be out before daybreak heading for the deer woods. Literally an army of men get out of their cars and make a drive on foot for a possible shot.

This action will without doubt put the game on the move. The man who picks himself a favorable stand early in the morning and stays there patiently is more apt to get a good shot at deer than the man who is doing the driving. Driving is exactly what this army of hunters is doing whether they know it or not. They are doing the driving for *you*. That's something to think about.

Patience is the keynote. Make your plan before season, pinpoint a strategic spot on a fresh run, and then wait. Pick a trail, or a place where trails meet, and hold it. Your stand must be strategic. There must be some conspicuous landmark present that draws the deer to it. And you must keep hidden.

I like to find a good spot to sit and wait. I must be warm and dressed for the weather. That's all-important. Then I want to be concealed with a clear view of the runway, facing upwind with rifle ready. I know of one expert who likes to stand with his back to a big tree. Most hunters like to sit just within the edge of the cover for an unobstructed shot. Determine from which direction the game is coming and face that way; but also watch for the wind. *It must be blowing from the game to you* if you expect a decent shot.

Many hunters have their stands picked out from previous years. This method is usually reliable, for deer use the same runs year in year out if they are not unduly molested. The best way to pick your stand is to do some scouting around just before deer season. Tracks will show at any time, and prominent landmarks will always be there. All summer long deer have been using these runs. Will they travel here during deer season? Chances are that they will, but you'll never know until you make a pre-season survey.

The moment of truth comes, however, when the big

day dawns and you plant yourself on that stand. Dress for the weather, I repeat; be warm, really warm, and then sit or stand quietly. Avoid any movement, and remember that each minute you wait becomes more significant, more promising, more precious.

You'll hear a shot here and there, and you'll be tempted to move. Assure yourself that time spent on that stand is on your side, and will bear compound interest. Sooner or later in reputed deer cover a deer will show. Keep alert, and watch for that tell-tale flick of a white tail, that tawny side of a deer, or any suspicious sound that signifies a deer. Sit tight and you'll win out. Too many times I have left my stand prematurely and returned to find fresh tracks nearby.

Stand-hunting takes fortitude. A confirmed trail watcher with this ability is a certain local shopkeeper acquaintance of mine. He is a deer hunter with much patience. One season this nimrod hunted three days at a favorite stand before he got his deer. Once he hunted a whole week before connecting. But he did come back with venison.

As hunting from a stand can be a tiresome procedure under some conditions, it is imperative to pick out a favored place where deer will show themselves. Where the country is dry the deer will head for watering places early in the morning. In the snow country the watering places hold little value because the deer can slake its thirst almost anywhere. But the spot must be interesting to you, the hunter, to be of value.

I have found that the rougher the country, the better.

The game heads for these areas, and will steer its course through them by conspicuous landmarks along the way. The deer will follow the natural lay of the land, keeping to the trails much of the time—especially early in the morning—and using certain runways. Make sure there are fresh tracks at a favorite stand and spend some time there.

Trail-watching can be an art or a chore. It can be both interesting and productive at the right place—one that you like. There is always something new to be seen. Always you are looking for deer, but at the same time you can observe the wildlife and the scenery.

The hunter may not have seen many grouse during bird season; now they seem to reveal themselves as they re-group for winter. There may be squirrels, ravens, or even a snowshoe rabbit—the latter just the thing for camp meat.

Always there will be the grand suspense of waiting for that deer. You must be quiet and persevering, and you must memorize every feature of the surroundings. You must be ready and alert. You will hear other hunters working the cover both near and afar; but you must hold to this spot and watch. The longer you stay there the better your chances are. The law of averages is working in your favor.

If the run has produced for you during other years, you will feel more at home there. Your odds of scoring are much more favorable. Location is all important. Make sure of deer signs around the place, like fresh tracks, droppings, and forage. Determine where the deer are bedding and where they are lounging. Pinpoint your spot and get there early. Make sure you can see a deer approaching, and then sit tight.

Many hunters have a path beaten from camp to some prime deer crossing. Every morning during season, even before breakfast, one or more of the hunters will be posted at this promising spot. Some hunters even place their camp right *on* a game trail, and watch from the window or door. The idea is to find the right spot, near camp or away from it, and watch, watch, watch.

With many hunters hiking through the woods your chances of seeing a deer are very good. I recall an instance when gunners were roaming about in numbers, and whether they knew it or not were actually driving game my way. I had hiked slowly down an old logging trail, and finally reached the edge of a swamp and a place where the runway entered it. It was early morning and a bit hard to hunt because a light snow was falling. But this was deer cover, a new slashing logged last year, and not too far off the main road. I had dressed for the occasion, and was hopeful since this cover had yielded two bucks on previous occasions.

There was a hunting camp not too far away, and I had no sooner found a hidden stand when I heard hunters near the camp shouting to one another that they had seen a deer. Evidently something was in the wind, and I faced the camp and waited. Several cars were parked near the camp and hunters were roaming the woods for some distance around.

This was one morning I did not have long to wait. The

footing was noisy, and I had no sooner gotten myself seated and comfortable than I heard a swishing sound in the brush, and the slight cracking of twigs. A doe and a fawn broke cover, and as I watched through the thin brush they moved along the edge of the swamp and then entered the woods not far from me.

Gripping my rifle I was now watching for the buck, and near the spot from which this pair emerged I caught a glimpse of antlers in the pale November light. It *was* a buck. As he came to an opening he surveyed the cover suspiciously, listening, testing the wind. Apparently he was on the trail of the doe and the fawn. It was not a long shot. Just as the buck threw all caution to the winds and broke cover, I held high on the shoulder and put the bullet right where I wanted it. No need for a second shot.

Infinite patience is needed for successful trail-watching. To sit quietly and alone for some hours at a stretch requires determination of a sort many hunters lack. But the secret of success in this game is just that. You must wait and sweat it out, if you will, until a deer nears your stand. There will always be the temptation to move along and find a better location. Doubts as to the wisdom of this place and this method of hunting will assail you from time to time. You've got to sit tight for success, and you must remind yourself of this plan at all times.

The law of averages is on the side of the man who sticks it out. All the time the hunter is on stand there will be hunters pressing through the cover, moving game. Why not take advantage of it? You won't get the physical action of these drivers, but sooner or later you should get a shot at game these men are pushing out.

Some hunters make a fire to keep warm, but this action is fatal to success at a stand. The basic strategy of trail-watching is sitting or standing quite motionless. Since a deer is color-blind, the hunter can even be stationed somewhat in the open and still be undetected by the game if he remains motionless and is upwind of the quarry. A deer's eyes are quick to detect motion in the brush. Some hunters wait until the deer is within some 20 feet of them before they raise their rifle.

Close range shots can best be obtained when the hunter stands off to the side of the trail, facing the possible approach of the deer. Once started a deer watches its backtrack more acutely than what lies ahead, which also affords the stand hunter a distinct advantage. Before the deer comes into an open crossing area it will usually stop and look around, affording the motionless hunter a fine chance for a shot.

Hunting from a stand is productive, and worthwhile. It may entail a long wait, be muscle-cramping and hard on the patience, but it will pay off in the long run, and is a boon to the lone hunter, especially. When he finds a choice spot and holds to it, sooner or later a deer will appear. He must resist any temptation to move. Time is definitely on the hunter's side, and the game will be coming along when he least expects it. He must be prepared for that magic moment.

If you have time, take your shot from the fairly steady kneeling position

Savage 99-F

Remington 760 ADL;
high-power slide-action repeating rifle

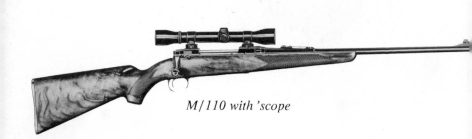

M/110 with 'scope

A buck in summer velvet, Jasper National Park, Alberta, Canada

Patient trail watching, rifle at the ready

Snow allows quiet stalking and tracking

Successful northern Michigan hunters bagged these four bucks

A sturdy well-heated wall tent makes comfortable quarters for on-the-spot deer hunting

Wisconsin white-tailed buck on the margin of his second-growth bailiwick

8
Stalking and Still-Hunting

BAGGING YOUR DEER BY A QUIET STALK, and on your own, is one of the highest achievements the hunter can aim for, especially when the game is resting in a carefully concealed bed. This is one form of deer hunting in which the deer has all the advantages, for this animal selects a position where it can watch all approaches; and it beds down where it has several escape routes available.

To take a deer by still-hunting is not an accident; it is an action which must be the result of the hunter's studied efforts. He must make use of all his hunting skills to approach within shooting distance.

One of the definite requirements of successful stalking and still-hunting is determining the usual resting places

57

for the deer. As soon as daylight breaks the game heads for its favorite bedding grounds. Like so many wild animals the white-tailed deer prefers to do its feeding in the early evening, the night, and the early morning. It takes its so-called leisure during the daylight hours.

In the daytime, then, the deer seeks seclusion, and will usually head for rugged and brushy terrain.

When the hunter goes about his still-hunting, it is wise to select a range with which he is familiar, and once there to make sure that the deer inhabit the area. If the country is worthwhile the deer tracks will show fresh and clear at the time of the hunt. The big consideration is to become acquainted with the range first, and then determine specifically where the deer travel, feed, and bed down.

Now the hunter should make the most of his findings, selecting productive cover and working it well. It is best to start at a specified point and follow the trails. There will be a certain direction taken by the deer in their travels, and this should be discovered and taken into account. Mostly, I have found, the white-tailed deer will head into the wind. By moving so the scent is in his favor, his keen sense of smell will enable him to detect danger for some distance.

Along the general travel routes there will be resting and bedding grounds. Although a deer may lie down and rest in a fairly open place, this is the rare exception. I have never moved a deer that was lying down in the open on the trail. More than once I have seen deer not more than ten feet from the trail, but always hidden in the brush.

Deer seem partial to low ridges just off the main deer runway. When lying on some small rise the animal can take off almost like a projectile, and will usually depart from its bed the way its shoulders are pointed. All too often the animal will have seen, scented, or heard the hunter first unless the latter has been very cautious in his approach.

There will be certain indications, like fresh tracks and brushy terrain which indicate the presence of deer. Silence and stealth are imperative. See your deer first, and for once place the odds in your favor.

Wind direction must be taken into full account. Let it blow from the deer you are stalking to you, and then plan to travel quietly. You must move slowly. The hurried rifleman may see deer at a distance, but the quarry will usually have seen him first and moved out. By making a quiet stalk the hunter can take into account wind direction and can see objects better as he travels than the man who is hiking at a good clip through the woods.

In suspicious territory be ready for a shot. Be doubly cautious, especially when working through the brush. For example, if a log blocks the trail, it's better to walk around it or slide over it than to step on it and jump down. On one occasion I had accomplished a successful still-hunt until I came to a heavy deadfall in a grove of evergreens. Instead of sliding over the log I stepped up on it and jumped down, sending a large buck flying into the hemlock thicket before I could effect a shot from my awkward position.

In this case, as it turned out, I was following the tracks of a male deer. This deer's print, like others of the male deer, toed out in the distinctive swagger of the buck, and the front feet were blunt and rounded. A doe's front feet usually point straight ahead, and are narrower than a buck's.

The size of the track is some indication of the deer's sex, but not much. If the track measures over three inches this might designate a buck. But again it may not, for there are some very large does in the deer range. A male deer has an entirely different carriage than a doe, however, and this rolling gait can be seen in the trail the deer makes.

More than once, even in winter when the deer are without antlers, I have been able to identify the buck by his carriage. The male deer has a blocky gait, a swing and a swagger that is far different from the mincing walk of the doe. Mostly, too, the buck is a loner.

When stalking this deer make sure the track is fresh, and then track the deer to his daytime hideout which is always in a different location from his nocturnal cover. Be extremely cautious, moving slowly, for always the deer is hiding out and watching, trying to evade predators of all types.

Stalking your buck to his bed along these routes has its merits. With a certain caution and care it can be done, not only once, but time after time. The secret is to find a promising runway and keep on it, making certain that the tracks you follow are fresh. It is also advisable to travel against the wind, which in this case, is usually on the track of the game, avoiding contact with foliage and brush.

Shortly you should spot your deer. If the tracks are there you can work your way through brush of all kinds, and sooner or later make a find. A quiet approach is essential, using the woodsman's mode of travel, which is not the stiff-legged heel-and-toe gait of the pavement, but the slightly knee-bent walk with the ball of the foot touching the ground first.

The idea is to be relaxed in all body movements, to keep the eyes on the scenery round about, and to steal in on any deer without its knowledge. This is entirely possible even when traveling at a fair rate of speed, if you are a skilled stalker. The novice is urged to move slowly, however, and always remain alert to anything that remotely resembles a deer. The average deer is not tall, seldom measuring more than 36 inches from its back to the ground. Most of the time the whitetail is hidden by foliage, so the stalker must look for something suspicious, rather than a whole deer. In autumn, too, the pelage takes on a grayish-tan cast, rendering the whitetail inconspicuous. The coat may not show up, but always the whitetail will have its "flag" as a dead giveaway. The tail usually stands out when the animal is moving.

When stalking a deer the hunter must also take into consideration that when a whitetail does bed down it does so in such a position that it can watch all approaches. Before it stretches out, the deer will move along in a wavering, uncertain manner, then face into the wind. The deer's sense of smell is very keen. As it knows that its natural enemies will be stalking along its trail, it turns that way before bedding down.

There will be something appealing to the deer about the spot of its choosing; in fact, it may seek the same place day after day. When not molested the deer travels very little, in an area usually not more than a mile square.

Hilly country is a preferred hideout for the first part of the season, anyway. Three deer I have in mind in the last few years chose a hidden spot where they could lie on a small incline, front feet downhill, ready for a speedy escape. Two of them got away. The first deer was lying behind a brush pile, well hidden. I had just left my hunting companion after lunch to make a drive on my own. Not long before, we had chased a buck and a doe across a small swamp with no chance for a shot, and somehow I had an idea that the buck was heading for a certain hill not too far distant. After leaving my partner, who had another area in mind for hunting, I headed north up a long hill, recently logged, and had almost topped it when I heard a couple of grouse clucking near a brush heap.

I had no idea a deer was anywhere around. However, I stole over to see what the commotion was all about and a whitetail crashed out ahead of me. Stepping onto the pile of springy brush, I somehow lost my balance and caught the merest glimpse of antlers. As the deer bolted, kicking gravel in my face, I shot from the hip but missed clean. That was the last I saw of that deer. I had no idea where he went and didn't try to follow.

The second deer that afternoon was as lucky as the first. The deer was lying in a hilly, wooded area and bounded into a thicket before I could even get a good aim. I had noted fresh tracks on a certain trail that also wound uphill, and I followed it slowly and cautiously.

This trail and this area in general was one of the best I'd run into all season, and one in which I'd hunted grouse successfully. Scouting the same area next day after a light snowfall, I managed to put in a telling shot. On the alert from fresh tracks in the snow, I played my hunch, stalked this brushy trail very quietly and carefully, and jumped this 6-point buck not 10 feet from the trail.

There may be some bedding grounds which are almost impossible to stalk successfully, but when the hunter knows that deer are in the vicinity he can wait until they leave these beds. Toward dusk they will begin a tentative feeding schedule, and then will move out toward their nighttime grounds. I must admit I've had little luck by waiting for them this way, but I do know of many hunters that follow this procedure each season with a fair degree of success. They have discovered deer by stalking; when the deer move out the hunters find a strategic stand and wait it out. This is combining stalking with runway-watching.

This type of hunting is not as surefire as stalking, but it does prove out time and again. It is a fine way to hunt just at dusk, especially if the nimrod carries a scope sight on his rifle for aid in sighting and "picking up" light.

In my case I like to cut a fresh print and then follow it.

I may pursue old tracks to see *how* the deer are covering the range, but when I want real action I find a new spoor and follow it up. This calls for tracking snow as a real incentive, but if a deer has been around it usually leaves some sign even on dry ground.

Moving slowly, I always walk as though a deer were just ahead of me, searching the vicinity all around for any sight of game, keeping my eyes on the scenery rather than my feet.

A whitetail is always suspicious of its backtrack so it is best to steal in from behind or from the side of the suspicious area.

One morning just after I had left my car, I met a hunter who had used this ruse to bag his buck in a stand of maple, within easy dragging distance from the main road, and in a downhill direction. He informed me as I met him that a woodsman friend of his had suggested this deer area. Starting in to the newly cut hardwood slashing before clear daybreak, this hunter had spotted four deer making their way through the open of the slashing. One of the group was a trophy buck.

As usual, the buck detached itself quickly from the rest of the group when the hunter approached, and somehow disappeared in the heavy brush at the edge of the cutting. Losing the trail at this point and at last relinquishing the chase temporarily, the hunter drove some distance to a Lake Superior coffeehouse, treated himself to a second breakfast, and then returned to resume the chase.

With broad daylight on his side, the hunter picked up

the track of the whitetail where he had left it, and shortly walked into a hardwood thicket where the tracks led him. Making a roundabout approach he spotted the buck lying in a small clearing. It was an easy shot with a deer that "just stood up and looked at me," as this man explained. He had his deer for the season.

It was a simple procedure, and a successful one. Stalking in from a different direction than the one from which the whitetail had entered, there was no speedy getaway— just a surprised deer and a successful stalker who knew where his deer lay and took fine advantage of it. This happy nimrod was cleaning his deer when I met him, whistling to warn other hunters not to shoot at him or his downed deer, as he explained it. In no time at all, with a little assistance from me, he had the beautiful 12-pointer field-dressed and tied to his car, and was on his way home just as I was starting my day.

Successful deer stalking demands determination and skill, in about equal amounts. The whitetail has his defense system worked out, but the hunter can beat the deer at this game if he learns the animal's little tricks and subterfuges.

The hunter must determine first where the whitetail spends its leisure time, where it beds, especially, and then approach with the idea of bagging the deer. He must spot the animal first, or at least quickly. It will pay him to stop often and study the surroundings quietly as he makes his stalk. He must suspect anything not quite part of the scenery.

When a whitetail is feeding, the hunter may have an

advantage, and find it easier to stalk. This is partly because of the feeding motions, but even here caution must be exercised.

Successful stalking of the whitetail deer might prove a bit difficult for the novice, but there is no reason that even the lowly beginner cannot succeed at the sport. He must be watchful, alert, and—above all—quiet. Nor is this method of hunting hard to achieve. It is often a fairly easy procedure because it is so fascinating and efficient. It is an Indian-like activity of the first water that will prove rewarding time and again.

9

Group-Hunting
(The Drive)

MORE THAN ONCE when seeking a certain deer the hunter can use a helping hand in making a drive. For instance when a deer has been sighted with two in the party, one of the men stays on the trail while the other makes an intercepting action, getting ahead of the animal and cutting it off. In this case the whitetail would be more suspicious of the man trailing than the one making a round-about maneuver.

Just as in any other drive, both men must keep in mind that they are working as a team, not as individual hunters. Should the deer fail to show up at the expected place, this "scout" tries to intercept the quarry at another point or rejoins his companion and plots another course of action.

Some hunters can work together very successfully. They contact each other from time to time, plan their action, and keep on a trail for a long period of time without fatigue. What's more, they bring game to bag.

There is no question that the lone hunter derives much satisfaction from his independent action, but at the same time two hunters can cover more ground than one, and are better able to round up any game that is jumped. For that matter many hunters will not hunt alone, in which case their best means of bagging deer is to work together with planning and organization.

There is a certain feeling of independence in hunting alone, a fine sense of elation in bagging a whitetail by oneself. But hunting with a partner is also a very pleasant and profitable way of deer hunting, especially when both men are skilled at the sport and can work together amicably.

The idea is to bring more deer within range of one gun or the other, and to move more deer than would be possible with only one man in the cover. If the partners travel within sight and sound of each other the elements of noise and scent are in their favor. In such hunting they should space themselves from 50 to 100 yards apart, depending on the density of the cover. Should game be moved thus there is every likelihood that it will be seen by both hunters. One man can also stalk the quarry and the other intercept it.

It is essential for success to determine how the deer move in the area, just as in a large drive, and then try to push the deer in that direction with your partner at a spot where the deer will most likely appear. Deer will move out of their hiding places if they are driven, and this often means just following in the fresh tracks of a deer or two. With an alert partner up ahead on a newly made track there should be action, and perhaps shooting.

When we think of driving deer, however, we think of driving by large groups, such as fifteen to twenty men, with the basic purpose to push deer up ahead to predetermined vantage points at which standers are located. Usually the drive is planned by someone well-versed in the art of driving deer and with an intimate knowledge of the deer range.

The number of men doing the driving should not be excessive, but they should travel near enough to each other to keep in contact. They should work to keep the game moving ahead and prevent them from cutting back.

The whitetail deer is reluctant to leave his hideout but will try to get away from the drive. Most of the time, however, if the general escape route of the deer has been considered, driving is quite successful and will keep the game moving ahead to the place where the watchers are stationed. Care must be exercised by the drivers so that they do not get any other hunters in their line of fire should they spot a deer. Really their main concern is to drive the deer into range of the watchers.

Again the essence of the whole action is teamwork. The drivers must keep up with each other, at an even pace, and try to push the game close enough to the line of watchers so that shooting will result.

The drivers will usually outnumber the watchers two

to one. The "key men" in the drive are the two hunters who hold down the end of the line. At these two points the driven deer will have the best opportunity to turn away and escape. The key men must try to guard against this, and like any of the other drivers, can shoot at any escaping deer.

Only a small area should be hunted in the drive, and when this cover has been worked thoroughly there is always the possibility of driving another promising piece of range. If the drive is small and well organized, and deer are in the vicinity, there should be shooting. It pays to study the natural escape routes of the game, which are usually into the wind.

An easier means of driving, often successful, is the action where the hunters fan out parallel to each other, with no standers involved, and try to bag any game encountered. Such a drive can be organized and carried on with a minimum of preparation and planning. For instance, there may be a small piece of thicket or swamp which has been found to hold deer from time to time. Fresh tracks show on the day of the hunt. The small party of hunters gathers on some logging trail, spacing themselves about 100 feet apart, and push through the deer habitat at an even pace.

If the deer are around, they will move out ahead of the hunters. More often than not they will present a fair chance of a shot. This is pretty much on the order of the pheasant-hunting drive, and is about as effective in good game cover. The deer will move. How far ahead of the drivers one can hardly predict; but move they will and provide action and shooting.

The old time deer drive was a noisy affair with the participants beating pans, ringing bells, shooting their rifles, and raising bedlam in general. There is no question that this ear-filling din put the deer on the run, and that many deer were bagged in the process. But the trouble with this action is that the deer will usually go out fast, and present nothing but fleeting shots.

When the drivers steal along quietly, not only will they have a chance to get a shot at the moving deer, but the deer will be easier to spot by all concerned.

The deer drive is particularly effective in the more populous eastern areas where only shotguns are permitted on deer. With buckshot, especially, the running deer is more easily taken with the shotgun, and being a short-range weapon, this firearm offers better safety precautions.

Whatever the firearm used, however, one of the main considerations in driving is to find the best places to hunt, and then to become familiar with the area. Numerous short drives are often more successful than one or two long ones, especially when the wind is not too constant. When much snow is in prospect, the game will often be in the swamps, and the idea is to select a small swamp and hunt it well. The short drive will last about 30 to 40 minutes, and if the area is well covered by the drivers, will move deer quite consistently if the game is there.

Other areas worth hunting are the small brush patches

and thickets such as are found through the farming country of western Pennsylvania. When the hunting season is still young, and many deer hunters are combing the woods, some of the wisest old bucks will leave their regular hangouts and hide out in the heavier thickets. There may be only one buck in the area, but chances are that this trophy will be well worth the effort of several small drives.

The trend toward group hunting is growing, and constitutes a hunting method that spells companionship. Working together as a unit and a close-knit team the hunters take game quite consistently.

10
Whitetails and the Weather

SINCE THE WHITETAIL DEER owes its very existence to its ability to foretell the weather and act accordingly, it will change its habits from time to time in direct ratio to what its sixth sense seems to dictate. I have seen mild, sunny days in the deer district when deer movement was especially apparent, and for no good reason that I could ascertain at the time.

During the daytime when the deer were supposed to be bedding down they would be traveling about, restless and jittery, feeding extensively instead of lying around in their hidden covert.

At such times I have sighted them in the clearings, on the trails, along the ridges, and in the slashings. They were much more actively engaged than on the previous day, and offered more than one chance for the observant deer hunter.

I discovered that after these days the weather had a way of changing overnight. One day the game was there, and the next it had vanished from the scene. Coincident with the decrease in deer activity I have usually noted a drop in the barometer.

I recall one season particularly when the game changed its habits to a marked degree, and certainly resulted in a decreased deer kill. During grouse season I had seen deer signs in a hilly area, a sort of pie-shaped district between two converging trails, and a place with enough cover to afford excellent daytime shelter for any number of animals. The deer had a habit of moving into this old slashing early in the morning, staying there most of the day, feeding a bit, but mostly resting.

This place had produced unusual hunting for two years previously and it still looked like productive habitat, a surefire hot spot.

On the day of my pre-season scouting trip I had no sooner turned off the main logging trail and into an offshoot than I heard several deer break cover and run ahead of me. The trail was literally cut up with animal tracks. As I rounded a bend and looked into a small clearing, I counted six deer working along the edges, in none too much of a hurry to move when they caught sight of me.

Later that day with the sun still bright and the air clear, I made a drive into a nearby area where the loggers were still working, and at one place ran across another concentration of whitetails. There were two mature bucks in this group which showed signs of nervousness and moved out when I moved in; but the rest did not seem unduly alarmed when I appeared on the scene, and I approached several of them at close range.

On the way back I sighted at least five other deer, not too far distant, and they all seemed busy in feeding. None was too disturbed as I hiked through the cover.

I met three hunters heading for their camp, all of whom had seen many deer. All remarked on how good the hunting would be the next day, which was the opener.

The next day was another story, however. Just at dusk it began to rain, the rain turned into snow that continued all during the night and well into the next day. When the storm abated there was a good foot and a half of the white stuff on the ground. Somehow the game had taken to cover and there were no tracks to be found in their usual feeding and lounging grounds.

The deer kill for the next two days was negligible, tracks were hard to find, and it was not until the third day of season that deer hunters reported any kind of success. In fact, many of the out-of-state and down-state hunters, the tent and trailer campers, especially, pulled out and returned home.

By the fourth day the weather moderated, much of the snow disappeared, and the deer were back in their regular range again, with tracks fresh and apparent most everywhere.

With their built-in sense of predicting the weather, the

animals had taken advantage of the good days to fill their bellies. And as soon as the severe weather abated they were at it again, picking up where they left off, and making up for lost time.

The whitetail is very sensitive to weather changes. You may be able to find deer even during severe weather, since the game does not vanish from the face of the earth, but good hunting is the exception at such times. In bad weather the whitetails will head for heavy cover, usually the swamps, and other places in the colder regions where the snow is not so deep. Even here, however, the game will be hard to find since they will be moving little.

There is never any reason for the dedicated deer hunter to give up, weather notwithstanding. His main concern is to find the game, and this is where sign reading enters the picture.

To illustrate, after one big snowstorm, and concentrating on one area, I was having little luck spotting game when I happened to run into another woodsman who lived in the vicinity. I had seen deer sign here and there, but nothing exciting. I teamed up with this native for a short while and he pointed out the game trend. They were moving into the places where the snow was not so deep, feeding in the more open spots. It was not long before we ran into one place were fresh tracks crossed and criss-crossed the slash, with clear evidence of deer movement.

About this time we decided to split up, and not more than a half hour later I heard a single shot not far away.

Following it up I found my erstwhile companion busily engaged in cleaning a good-sized buck.

This buck was a solitary one, but not long after that, after helping my new-found companion haul his deer to camp, I ran across several others, always at a distance.

These deer were holding out not far from a grassy clearing, and seemed to be moving considerably. Throughout the day I caught sight of several other deer, mostly of the antlerless variety, however, and always at a distance. The bucks, as usual, managed to keep under wraps much of the time, but all through this area where the snowfall had been only slight the game was traveling freely. Tracks were fresh and easy to follow.

Even when the weather is at its worst the serious hunter can still bag game. At one time our party of three picked up a track of a solitary buck in kneedeep snow and tracked it to its bed, a grove of dense hemlocks that provided shelter. From all appearances we gave this mature whitetail buck the surprise of its life when we finally jumped it from its dry bed under the trees, and the man in the lead lifted his rifle.

Another time during a snowstorm a woodsman friend of mine had hunted all day hard and faithfully to come away empty-handed. However, with the snow still falling, and when driving home along the highway, he saw a good-sized buck standing near the road sheltered by tall trees. Getting out of his car the man dropped it then and there. Again, after a very heavy snowfall I made a short drive along a trail with not a sign of a deer until I started into the heavier woods, when a buck and a doe appeared out of nowhere, much to my surprise. The buck was gone before I could even raise the rifle, but I had sighted deer, and proved to myself they were still around.

The hunter, like the quarry, should take account of weather conditions, and try to get in his licks when the game is most active. There is never any use in giving up, however. If the tireless hunter keeps at it, sooner or later he may rate the shot he's been banking on.

11
The
Rutting Moon

IN THE LATE FALL the rutting season is on. It is a time when the shy and retiring buck of the summer becomes much more aggressive. Consumed with the fever of breeding, the buck is on the prod. He sharpens his antlers to polished tines by rubbing them against bushes and trees, and is ready to have it out with any other buck invading his domain.

This burning urge may lead the buck to change his routine somewhat. He's up and traveling earlier in the morning, and may roam widely far into the night, searching for a willing doe. On several occasions I have seen beautifully antlered bucks, especially on moonlit nights, far out of their usual bailiwick. One night, as I was traveling along in a car, I saw one running across an open field, free as the wind. On another occasion, also in my car, I saw one on the outskirts of a large town, pausing briefly on an elevated railroad track to take in his surroundings, and then move elsewhere.

Mostly the bucks hold to their native habitat, where they may meet a potential competitor, often with disastrous results.

When this encounter occurs one or the other of the male deer may back away, but more than likely they will meet head on with a mighty crash of antlers and fight to the end, their antlers locked in mortal combat. They push and gouge, twist and strain with mouths agape, tearing up the sod with their hoofs as they lunge at each other. If one of the bucks can break loose he may either bore in again at the other buck's head, or try to strike him sidewise in a wild charge.

It often happens that the antlers become locked as the fight continues, and sooner or later both deer are down for the count, still struggling, their antlers twisted in a hopeless tangle. Instances have occurred when one buck had his neck broken in the struggle and the other was unable to extricate himself. The winner may starve to death or be claimed by some hunter who may happen along.

What usually occurs, however, is that the lesser buck may break away after a few minutes of combat, leaving the field to the stronger of the two.

This combat may or may not be for the affections of some nearby doe. I have witnessed two such fights when there was no other deer present. The paths of the two bucks seemed to cross in a casual encounter and they went at each other with hammer and tongs. When I put in my appearance they promptly pulled apart and vanished in the brush. On one of these occasions I did see a doe on the outskirts of the battleground, but from what I could gather she was merely a disinterested spectator, and the object of the fight was to drive the weaker male out of the area rather than to win the affections of the doe.

In the northern whitetail range the peak of breeding activity occurs early in November, but in the southern range it tends to happen later. The buck is sexually mature at about one-and-a-half years of age, while the doe can be successfully bred the first fall after it is born.

A buck may stay in breeding condition from about September through February, but not always will he find a receptive doe. The doe's heat period lasts only 24 to 36 hours. She reaches that condition again in about 28 days if not successfully bred the first time.

The doe has three such periods possible during the breeding season, usually insuring that each doe will be bred and rear a fawn in the spring. There is little indication anywhere in the whitetail range of a breeding buck shortage. Even where the bucks are none too plentiful there is a fawn crop every year, for in the wild a buck can usually service from six to seven does during the season, and as many as twenty when penned up in a semi-tame state.

Just when the rut will occur is not always possible to

accurately forecast, but it does often coincide with the hunting season. In this regard, experts say that it is the waning light of the fall that brings on the rut, not frost or change in temperature as is commonly thought. In the north woods, as noted, the mating season comes in late fall, but it also may occur as early as September.

At this time the buck may be in an amorous mood, but not always the doe. She may not be receptive to the buck until about ten days after he enters the rut, and at this time the buck is particularly aggressive, and where possible will usually be close to some doe, following, or taking the lead, as the case may be. During this season, especially, the hunter should take heed of any congregation of does, or even a single doe, waiting and watching. If he does not see a buck close at hand, sooner or later one will usually appear.

All this points to using a commercial scent to attract deer. If this scent is based on sexual attraction, and is properly prepared and used, it should be effective. One of the most popular is that taken from the inner side of the back leg glands of a doe. This is rubbed on the clothing. This musk is particularly strong, hiding not only human odor, but producing a scent that bucks can detect and will often follow.

Other aids to attracting deer are deer calls, but I doubt very much their efficacy. I have heard what sounded like the cry of a fawn during the hunting season, but I couldn't prove that it was a fawn. Even if it was, such a cry would only attract the doe for which it was looking.

As a rule, the fawn is pretty well grown during the hunting season, and on its own much of the time.

Another method of attracting deer in certain parts of the country is the use of sticks or antlers rubbed together to sound like two bucks meeting each other head on. This method of bringing deer to hunters is often effective where the rutting season is fairly long, such as in Texas and New Mexico, and usually during the month of December. I have never seen it used in the north woods, nor even heard of it being used there.

For the rattling process, seasoned and dried out antlers are employed, and for the desired effect the hunter slams them together violently and twists them back and forth, trying to imitate the sound effects of an actual battle between two bucks. To simulate the fight between two large, belligerent bucks, heavy antlers are employed. They are struck together rather slowly, and with as much force as possible. To attract the smaller specimens lighter antlers are used, and they are banged together steadily and with a lighter touch.

Naturally, all this will have to be accomplished in an area where the deer will hear the sounds, which means reputed deer cover where there is an abundance of male deer. The sounds carry best on a cold, clear day, and the rattling is also most effective when the bucks are on the move. Rather early, that is, as well as toward evening when they tend to be heading out again from their bedding grounds.

The call is also best used in brushy country where the

deer cannot be seen unless they are approached rather closely. If the rattling of antlers is done effectively the bucks can often be lured into the open, or at least close enough to the hunter for a shot. Conditions will have to be close to ideal, however, for the effectiveness of this system. This means a high ratio of bucks to does. The country must be brushy, too, and the rattling must be done definitely during the rut.

12
Bullet Placement and Trailing Wounded Deer

VERY FEW DEER THAT ARE STRUCK by the rifleman's bullet will collapse on the spot. The best way to drop a deer instantly is to hit it with a neck shot at short range, or head on between the eyes. This kind of a target with the deer standing does not occur very frequently, but it is a good one. The bullet put between the eyes will penetrate the brain, while the one through the front of the neck will break the spinal cord, stopping the deer dead in its tracks.

Head-on shots are a possibility, but more than likely the deer will be moving and present a target from the rear. In this case the hunter can kill the animal instantly with a bullet through the spine, or one through the neck or head.

Needless to say these are small and difficult marks when the deer is moving rapidly. An easier target in such a case is the rump just at the base of the tail. If this mark is held on accurately by the rifleman the bullet will smash into the tip of the spine with almost instantly fatal results. Shooting into the rear of the animal may spoil a certain amount of meat, but it will also drop the deer very quickly and near at hand. And being a fatal shot it is humane; with this shot the deer will go down as though pole-axed.

Another fatal shot is the heart shot, striking just behind the shoulder and low in the chest. This will not drop the deer in its tracks by any means; the deer may keep on going for some distance. But sooner or later it will go down leaving a clear blood trail to follow. A bullet like this in the heart and lungs will sever large arteries and veins in that area. Where the deer is standing broadside to the hunter it is highly recommended.

Chances are the short-range neck-shot or the head-shot deer will drop on the spot, but even here it pays to keep your sights on the game and put in another shot if the deer does not quickly go down. Many hunters have lost their crippled deer because they failed to put in another finishing shot.

That is, the hunter shoots and sees the deer react violently to the shot; but when he reaches the spot where the deer was hit he sees no signs of the game. A second bullet would have done the trick and killed the deer cleanly. At any rate, when the hunter fires a well-held shot he should do his best to make a clean hit, and if he fails to drop the deer to keep an eye on the escaping animal and head for it at once.

It would seem that the heart-shot deer should go down quickly and fatally, but this is not always so. I have seen a young buck run for 300 yards with a direct heart shot from a .25-3000 caliber bullet. Had this been a brain or spinal cord shot the deer would have dropped then and there. A deer struck in the heart often explodes ahead in a wild burst of energy, desperate in its life tenacity, and may disappear in the brush and escape unless the hunter can follow its flight quickly and surely. This points up the fact that every shot should be followed.

The deer is relatively thin-skinned, fragile-boned, and highly nervous. But once this animal is spooked and running—even when hit—its energy seems to skyrocket. The animal may get away if not quickly trailed. When hit, then, the deer should be trailed at once. It may drop shortly or it may be lost in heavy brush, but you will never know unless you follow shortly.

Again one deer may drop quickly and another hang on with remarkable resistance. The size of the deer may have something to do with its life expectancy when shot, but usually it is the vigor of the deer which determines how quickly it will go down for good after being hit.

The buck in the prime of its sexual vigor may have a will to live and escape that is astonishing. The opposite is often true of the young deer, the quite old deer, and the does, animals that seem to go down with ease. This indicates that the age and the physiology of the animal have much effect on its demise when struck by the hunter's bullet.

Very rarely does the nervous whitetail offer anything but a running shot, and that from the rear. On this shot the hunter may line his sights on the big white tail and overshoot the escaping animal. As well, many running deer are missed by an error in leading. On the straight-away shot no lead will be necessary, but on the running broadside shot one must shoot ahead of the animal to connect. The trial-and-error method is one of the best teachers in the matter of leading, but there are certain rules which can be followed. Below is a table determining the lead when shooting a .30-30 caliber rifle with 170-grain bullets.

TABLE I

	Speed of Deer	
Distance to Deer	10 mi. pr. hr.	20 mi. pr. hr.
50 yards	lead 12 inches	25 inches
75 yards	lead 20 inches	38 inches
100 yards	lead 28 inches	52 inches

One of the difficulties with this table is judgment of the speed factor of the deer. It will help to remember that at 10 miles per hour the deer would be running rather slowly, while at 20 it would be in high gear and covering terrain in swift leaps and bounds. The hunter will try to take his shot whenever possible. However, if he is able to trigger when the deer is either at the top of one of its bounds, or when it strikes the ground, he will find his target most stable.

Any shot that downs a running deer will be a good one, no matter how fast the animal is traveling, or at what distance the shot is taken, unless very close. At all events, the hunter is urged to take a shot if it seems at all possible, for the hunter who waits for the "perfect" shot on whitetail deer will pass up most of them. This deer is almost always screened by brush and trees.

When hit, the running deer will usually stagger, but it may also accelerate its pace immediately afterwards. When struck in the front of the body it will often rear on its hind legs. When struck far in the rear of the body it may kick out wildly with both front legs.

There will always be some indication of a hit, but no matter how the deer reacts, head for the animal at once. Reload the rifle, all the while keeping your eyes on the place you last saw the deer. Then run out the shot. Trail it at once, and if you can't find the downed animal look for trail signs such as patches of blood, bits of hair, or other marks of wounding. The longer the hunter waits, the fainter the trail signs will be. The initial shock of a wounding hit may not be painful to the animal. It may weaken it, surely, but instinct will lead the animal to head for cover instantly.

Examine the trail and the surroundings thoroughly if the deer has not fallen within sight. The deer may not flinch at the bullet wound; it may not even drop its tail, or show signs of great distress. So head for it with rifle at the ready, and don't quit the trail until you've proved to yourself conclusively that the deer was not hit.

If the wound is sufficiently severe and the blood loss considerable the animal will go down close to where it was hit. If not, the thing to do now is to trail the wounded animal, marking the spot at which you wounded it.

One fallacy I have seen exploded is that a wounded deer will travel downhill in rough country. It may and it may not. A companion and I followed a deer that climbed a fairly steep hill even when bleeding profusely from a wound low in the chest. With snow on the ground the blood trail was clear and clean, and we finally cornered the wounded deer in a rough piece of logging slash, still up in the hill country.

By the way, this was the densest cover within easy reach, although the deer did follow a trail for a short distance when getting there. If there are two men following the wounded deer your chances of recovery are better than when hunting alone. But whatever the circumstances one must follow his deer with great care, holding tenaciously to what trail signs are present. The hunter will have to hunt and stalk this animal just as he would a normal deer, except that chances are it will weaken sooner or later. And when reaching dense cover by all means be ready for a quick shot, for the animal can hide out very close at hand.

The sooner the deer is found the better. The meat may become tainted if the wounded animal travels too far and too fast, and there is a possibility that darkness may put a stop to the trailing. If night falls by all means mark the spot you lost the deer and try for it the next morning. Recover the wounded animal if you can. Even the next morning the meat will be perfectly edible and fit for food unless the deer has been badly gutshot.

Wounding of game remains an unavoidable possibility. But persistent trailing can often help the hunter recover his deer; it is a necessary part of the hunting effort.

13
Venison

ONCE YOUR DEER IS DOWNED make sure that it is dead before making a close approach. More than one hunter has been attacked or injured by a "dead" deer coming to life. With rifle pointing at the animal, move in from behind and give it a shove with your foot. Wait for any reaction. If there are any signs of life put a bullet in the neck.

By all means don't rush in with your knife for the *coup de grâce*. One of my hunting companions suffered a severe gash in his arm when he started cutting into his deer, a wound that required medical attention at a town far from the scene of the accident. Another friend of mine put his deer down with a head shot, and walking in to investigate, saw the animal arise quickly and escape into the brush. His bullet had merely stunned the deer, striking an antler.

There is no need to bleed your deer unless the animal has been hit in the head, neck, or spinal cord. A wound in the lungs and heart, or through the body proper, will render bleeding unnecessary. If bleeding is indicated, plunge your knife at the junction of the neck and chest and cut down toward the backbone, being careful not to mutilate the carcass.

At this stage of the game take off your coat, roll up your sleeves, and begin the field-dressing. The viscera must be removed and as neatly as possible.

First of all make sure your knife is sharp, and then roll the animal on its back and into a position where the head will be higher than the hindquarters so the blood will drain to the hind parts. Insert your knife at the tip of the breast bone and split the skin down along the abdominal wall to the pelvic bone, being very careful to guide the knife so that it does not enter the paunch or intestines. To aid in this incision, use the fingers to press the internal organs away from the cutting edge of the knife. Now cut around the anus and remove the buck's reproductive organs.

This done, roll the animal on its side so the inner organs will protrude, and then loosen them from the abdominal wall by running the hand in between and cutting away the gullet. You may be able to remove the gullet with your hand, but cutting with a knife is a better means of separation.

Now bring the stomach outside the body with the intestines still attached. There should be enough room for the hunter to reach into the pelvic cavity and sever the lower intestine. Cut it away carefully with a tight grip on the intestine. Then remove the bladder, as well as any other matter which may be present, such as the diaphragm and the lungs.

Clean out the rectal area carefully by splitting the pelvis with knife or axe, and if much blood remains wipe it from the body cavity with rags or paper towels, using no water. With all blood and internal matter removed, the carcass will be ready for hauling. Field-dressing takes little time, even when thorough, and the sooner it is done the better.

Transporting the carcass can be easy or difficult depending on circumstances. One such circumstance would be the presence or absence of snow. You may even be able to drive your car or jeep right to the deer. If not, with or without snow, dragging is your best bet. In this operation first tie the forelegs back of the antlers, attach your drag line to the neck or antlers, and proceed to haul away the carcass. On snow you will find that the animal slides easily, providing the cover is not too overgrown or rugged in general.

One definite warning: don't carry out the deer on your back, or even tied to a pole in the two-man carry! This may be all the invitation some trigger-happy hunter needs to use the moving deer as a target and put you in his direct line of fire. It has happened; so the best method of moving your deer in the woods proper is by dragging, even when the ground is bare. What meat you might spoil will be negligible.

If your hauling takes you to camp, hang the deer high on the camp pole, and prop it open with two or three sticks so that internal heat will escape and the carcass will cool. This is important. If the weather is warm the deer should be draped with a cheesecloth or muslin to keep it safe from flies as well as birds that might attack the meat.

Hang the deer in a shady place, keep it cool, and when ready to leave camp place it in the partly opened trunk and keep it clean and untainted. You may want to display it on the fender, which will not damage the venison if the weather is not too warm or the trip too long.

The more help you can get in handling the carcass at this point, the better. Nothing is more of a dead weight than a limp, freshly killed deer. It has a way of slipping and sliding all over the place. If the weather is below freezing you will have little trouble in preserving the meat, but in warm weather it is a good plan to get the carcass home quickly once you leave, and to make the trip in the cool of the night or morning.

Once home, the deer should be kept in a cool place such as the garage. The next step is to skin and quarter the carcass, and then have it cut up into smaller sections, ready for the pan. Unless you like butchering, the best place for the venison now is your commercial locker. State regulations usually demand that the deer be skinned first. To do this start by splitting the hide along the back of the hind legs, then pull it away from the haunches and back, using one hand for pulling and the other for hammering the hide away from the flesh. You will have to use the knife occasionally to cut away the hide, but usually it can be pulled and "fisted" until you reach the forelegs where the knife will come into good use.

All this time the hunter is aiming for good-tasting meat, and one of the secrets of sweet venison, along with keeping it cool and clean, is the aging process. This aging should be done under controlled conditions. You can let the meat age in your garage, if it is cool, but it is better kept in a cold storage plant where you're sure it will be chilled properly at all times. You can start eating the venison within a week, but a two weeks' lapse of time between the shooting and the eating is recommended.

The hunter, too, can cut the meat into pan portions, not to mention wrapping it in packages, but your meat cutter will usually do a better job. Since he has the basic tools, a clean place to work, and the necessary qualifications, I'd say let him attend to this chore as much as possible. This will insure the meat reaching the table in prime, tasty, and easily handled portions.

Most hunters will want the venison processed into the conventional steaks, roasts, chops, ribs, and the like, with the tougher parts converted into hamburger. As well, some men like to use a good part of the meat for sausage, usually made by using one-third venison and two-thirds pork. It is then seasoned, ground, cooked, and stuffed into beef casings. All this can be done at home, too, but you will find that your local butcher will do the job better, especially if he is a man who specializes in sausage making.

From here on you will enjoy your venison—if you cook it properly—pretty much as you do beef. One of my favorites is swiss steak, and this is prepared the same as if it were beef. It tastes about the same, if not better, with that distinctive venison taste. For that matter, venison, if properly cared for and properly cooked, is delicious fare. You may want to add sauces or seasonings to give it that extra flavor, but this can be said about any kind of meat. A little care in the cooking will bring out the real taste, distinctly venison, and will help spread out the enjoyment of the hunt over a long period of time.

14

The Deer Camp

AT ONE TIME THE DEER CAMP consisted of either the tent or the permanent camp built of planks or logs. Nowadays it also includes the camper-trailer, the pick-up trailer, and the more commodious house trailer.

Each one has its advantages, but it's a fact that when you're camped right there in the field you'll see more deer. Some deer hunters prefer to stay at motels and hotels in the district, and this places them farther from the actual deer cover. But it can be a satisfactory arrangement.

Whatever the camp, and it need not be fancy, it should be practical and as near the game area as possible. There are any number of successful nimrods who are up at the crack of dawn and scouting some favorite game crossing. These men usually fill their tags each season, for the simple reason that they are right in the field, and put out that extra effort that is necessary in modern-day whitetail hunting.

There is nothing better than the permanent shelter for comfort, whether log or board. I started out my whitetail hunting ventures from such a camp. I recall how successful the hunting was and the relaxing and heart-warming times we enjoyed.

Naturally, it is not all hunting in the deer camp. It is also a time for good fellowship, especially during the evening hours. I remember several seasons at our camp on Lake Gogebic, in northern Michigan, when the place was crowded with friendly hunters. We managed to bag only a deer or two among us, but had a lot of fun in the process. The camp was situated on a beautiful lake, in superlative hunting territory, and we enjoyed the wonderful camaraderie of men who liked the outdoors.

To some deer hunters the camp is the thing, and to this end they go to some trouble and expense in obtaining a tract of land and building an adequate camp on it. Usually it is a board affair or a durable log cabin with logs cut right in the vicinity. Once the camp is constructed it will have to be checked and repaired from time to time, and firewood will have to be cut for the hunting season, all pleasant chores. One way to win an invitation to the deer camp for the season is to help keep it in firewood and lend a helping hand in general.

Many hunters who travel some distance to the deer

woods will set up camp in a tent or a trailer, and fare quite well if the weather is not too severe. A roomy tent, like a wall tent or an A shape, warmed with a wood-burning stove, can be a fairly comfortable shelter. It is used a lot in the deer woods. It is large enough to house several hunters comfortably.

Another practical tent is the more modern "pop-up" type. This tent is held up by an outside aluminum alloy frame, which does away with guy ropes and center poles. A tent of this type is so rigid and light that you and your partner can pick it up, still assembled, and move it, if necessary, to a more suitable site nearby. This type of tent can be obtained in sizes for one, two, three, or four men.

Other functional tents for cold weather are the explorer, the umbrella, the miner, the A tent, and the wall. In any of these, for the colder weather, I would suggest a ground floor, and a fairly heavy fabric. One of the roomiest and most practical for the stationary camp is the wall tent. This type lends itself nicely to a fly. It affords an insulation from above, and a protection against rain and snow, especially the latter.

If you have any choice in your camp site, the tent should be placed where it is sheltered from the wind in a brushy spot or a small clearing rather than in the big woods proper.

By all means make sure there are no large trees in the vicinity that can fall across the tent. Also try to find a spot protected from the wind and yet with as much warming sunlight as possible. If you can keep it near the car so much the better. This is usually possible.

More and more, however, the tent is being replaced by portable camp units such as fold-up tent trailers, pick-up campers, and house trailers. In the north woods I have noticed that the house trailer is in the minority, but I do know that where it can be used in the easily accessible areas it makes a very comfortable camp and one that will require a minimum of care during the hunting term.

I have found that the better the camp the better the frame of mind on the part of the hunters. Make sure of your bedding, in the nomadic camp, especially, and use an air mattress and a down-filled sleeping bag, or plenty of warm blankets. Go to any extent to assure yourself a good night's rest. Keep warm at all times, both with suitable clothing and sleeping gear.

You will also need a good supply of substantial foods and the wherewithal to cook it. One of the best stoves for the tent camp is the Swedish Primus portable stove that burns white gas, naphtha, or Coleman fuel. There may be times when you want to cook over an open fire, but there are also many times when the compact one-burner or two-burner portable stove can't be beat. By all means include it even if you have to backpack your supplies. An open fire has its romantic overtones, but this cooking does take a lot of precious time which may be better spent in hunting.

This points to another angle, and that is to use food items on the market that are easily prepared and are wholesome and nutritious. This suggests ham and bacon, with the ham the semi-boneless, fully cooked variety, and the bacon sliced. If the camp is far from the car, you can also include the freeze-dry foods, like Armour's Star Lite, which are lightweight and easily prepared. Make your evening meal a substantial and gala affair and you'll live like a king, especially if there is one man in the outfit who likes to cook.

The climate and weather conditions pretty much dictate the type of deer camp required. In New Mexico your deer camp would be much simpler and airier than your deer camp in northern Minnesota. In the south a tent on the order of the Baker with cots and light blankets might fill the need; but in the north where the temperature may drop close to zero during deer season, and where snow is the prospect, you will want a tight and warm sleeping quarters. You will want it heated by a stove, perhaps, and with bedding on the order of a down-filled sleeping bag, air mattress, and cot.

The day of the makeshift deer camp is pretty much a thing of the past, or should be. With modern camping conveniences now available, more time is spent in the actual hunting, and less in working around camp, trying to keep warm.

15
Survival and the Compass

WHEN A PERSON SUDDENLY FINDS HIMSELF mixed up, unable to decide which way the camp lies, his best recourse is to sit down and think it over. He should try to reconstruct the various moves he has made.

With rifle and ammunition, matches, warm clothing, and knife, a man can live off the country for days—if he is at all resourceful, and if it is necessary. This should be his assurance that there is no personal danger in becoming lost.

In most hunting areas a man will be able to supply himself with edible game should he need it. Not only that, but if he can keep himself under control, and stay in one place, he will surely be found by searching parties.

103

No sooner is a hunter reported lost than experienced woodsmen, usually under the direction of the sheriff's department or the conservation commission, are out *en masse,* looking for him.

However, if at all feasible, a man must try to work his way back to camp, or at least to some familiar landmark. He should first try the direction which seems most logical and keep on it until proven in error, *marking his way as he goes along.* He should return then to his starting point and begin anew, casting about in another likely direction, but not haphazardly. He must try to determine where the trail *ought to go,* searching for some likely opening which leads to familiar ground.

By observing the lay of the land, as well as consulting the compass, the lost hunter must try to exit the easiest way, without becoming involved in rugged terrain, *especially swamps.*

In traveling, select some landmark such as a tree, and make a beeline for it, and on reaching this spot, select another such landmark a short distance ahead and aim for that. Use the compass religiously here so as not to diverge from your objective.

Keep from getting lost in the first place by taking precautions as you hunt. Instead of detracting from the sport, this will add to it in that a man is always aware of his relation to camp and his position in general in the hunting district. Note landmarks, take account of changes in direction as you travel, and correlate them with the landmarks you run across.

With snow on the ground, the backtrack is simplicity

itself, for *the return is made along the trail previously laid*. A man's own track is his best guide, so he should keep on it carefully, and make sure that he can recognize it should it cross another hunter's track.

All precautions notwithstanding, however, let's consider the situation when a man does become lost. Relax. That is the watchword, although it is easier said than done. Try to still the feeling of panic which may arise. Sit down and think things out.

If a man can keep a close grip on himself the battle is half won. When lost, he is not so much endangered by his surroundings as he is by himself. Most lost hunters come out of the woods on their own power, unassisted. Perhaps a few spend a night in the woods, which, with a fire going, even in cold weather is no hardship. Any man fairly well clothed can stand a night or two, and more, if he knows how to keep warm. He can even find enough game to support him for quite a while if he goes about it rationally.

There is this consolation always: if you're that hunter and you're unable to find your way out on your own, you can be dead certain that other members of your hunting party, or a very efficient sheriff's department, will be looking for you. Your companions in the hunt will usually have a fairly good idea where you entered the woods, and in what area you were hunting. They can remember when you were last seen, at any rate, and be on the alert to get help when you fail to show up at a reasonable hour. From that time on you will be the object of an intensive search and will usually be found. If not that night, you will be found some time in the morning.

Always, of course, it is up to the lost hunter to help himself. The more evidence you leave of your presence, the easier for the trackers to unravel your trail. And this is certain: it will just hinder the searchers if a person wanders through the woods aimlessly. A man who is hopelessly lost and who builds a healthy fire for a signal and for heat will do himself and everybody concerned a good turn.

One of the worst eventualities of being lost is the prospect of darkness closing in. *Here again, make a fire.* A well-fed blaze will help lighten the scene and add cheer. Build it high and blazing. For one thing it will keep the woodsman occupied. For another, the smoke and flames from the fire will act as a beacon for spotting planes, or for men on foot, and chances are great the signal will lead the searchers to the lost man within a reasonably short time.

Also, by staying close to the place where he did lose the trail, the hunter, resting and "cooling off" a bit, may be able to think his way out. The fire is his camp site; it is a haven of sorts. The man who barges wildly through the woods is simply confusing the issue. If he will sit down for a time, various landmarks may occur to him, as well as other helpful details of the trip which will refresh his memory. This, and the use of the compass, may furnish him with a reasonable plan for reaching camp.

If the hunter is lost at night, which is usually the case, he should stick by his camp fire, and wait for daylight. At intervals, with enough shells, he can signal for help. During the stillness of nightfall a rifle shot carries a long distance and is noted by anybody within earshot. Three reports is a distress signal; but one shot, spaced at long intervals, may suffice to bring help.

With enough cartridges, the lost hunter can signal often, *but he must never use up all his shells!* Without his ammunition he'll have a hard time getting game to keep him alive. And above all else, he must never discard any part of his personal gear under the mistaken impression that he will travel faster that way, for this is the greatest fallacy of all. The hunter now has more need for his gear, clothing, rifle, and shells than ever before, so he must keep them intact, as well as to guard his match supply. *The matches are a life-saver, and must never be depleted!* Build the fire carefully, with one match to start it, if possible. And when in the woods always make sure you have a generous supply of waterproof matches with you at all times, and use them sparingly.

The lost hunter should build his fire close to water, if possible, and then rest, the sooner the better. The temperature during late fall, and even in winter, in most deer-hunting regions, is rarely so severe that a man dressed for it cannot endure a night or two out of doors if he builds an adequate fire and erects a shelter of sorts. The fire comes first, then the shelter—just a windbreak, if nothing else, or a backing of logs to reflect the heat. Then try to keep warm and rested.

A resourceful man can get along without an axe or knife, if he has to. Dry wood can be picked up almost anywhere in wooded area, even with snow on the ground. Look for the snap-brittle branches which grow near the base of evergreen trees. Many of them will break off easily and provide just the kindling needed to start a fire.

Even if things are wet and soggy a man can usually find sufficient dry wood, both to make a fire and keep it going. Besides dry branches, dry stumps may be available.

The hunter should start a good fire and erect a shelter of sorts, then make the best of it, staying with it until morning. By that time, with daylight on his side, he may be able to work back to camp. If still unable to do so he should maintain his vigil near the fire, keeping a smoke cloud rising, a signal which will eventually be spotted by plane or by rescuers on foot.

The lost man can then work out from his base camp, blazing a trail which he can backtrack if he has to. There will be more activity now. As the hunter travels he should halt occasionally and listen for sounds that indicate civilization—a rifle shot, an auto horn, a train whistle, the engine of a plane, the ring of an axe or chain saw, the bark of a dog, or a shout. If possible, he can climb some elevation and search for smoke or signs of habitation. If he runs across a stream, he can parallel it at a decent distance to get away from the thick brush. Certainly after traveling no more than an hour or two, he will surely find human habitation along its bank.

He can shoot game as he sees it, legal or otherwise, if he is hungry. Small game will usually evince itself, such as rabbit and grouse. He can carry it with him if he decides to keep on traveling. Chances are the lost hunter will suffer little harm from his mishap if he conducts himself rationally. He will, however, lose precious hunting time, not to mention peace of mind for himself and others, so he should not get lost in the first place! It can be avoided most of the time. If a man plans his hunt as he travels, makes mental notes and compass readings en route, he should hit camp smack-dab, right on the nose, and with little trouble. These little observations on landmarks, deviations from the main route, time of travel, time of day, along with a steadfast faith in the compass and an ability to follow its readings, will keep the hunter coming in from the trail fresh and relaxed, no matter what part of the hunting district he tackles.

Nor does a man have to be a born woodsman to accomplish this feat. There is nothing uncanny about this ability and nothing "instinctive." It is all based on common sense, a willingness to study and *recognize the surroundings as a man hunts,* and to keep cool and rationalize should the occasion demand it. The skilled hunter is always observant, always takes note of his directive travel, and *always uses the compass when he has to.* During the hunting season it may be a life-saver; keep one always in your pocket and know how to use it. Chances are you'll have no trouble at all in your woods travel.

16
Safety
with Firearms

AS LONG AS THE HUMAN ELEMENT is involved, hunting accidents will occur. Some are unavoidable, but most can be prevented. As compared to the number of riflemen who engage in the sport, accidents are not numerous. But they do tend to give deer hunting a bad name. One serious firearms accident in a community can do much damage to the morale and put all deer hunters on the spot.

With even less space to hunt than there used to be, and with more hunters using it, the solution is obvious: *be careful with your firearms.* Most hunting accidents are preventable. It is a personal thing. Take it upon yourself to play safe when hunting and you'll succeed.

The deer hunter must use his hunting equipment sensibly; it is not only for his own safety, but the safety of others, too. Adhere to the hunting code; gain respect and admiration among your hunting friends. The man who handles his sporting arms carefully is the man who will be well met in the outdoors fraternity. His firearms are dangerous, he knows this, and he handles them accordingly.

A good sportsman learns how to handle his gun with care. The accidental discharge happens mainly to the man who has had little experience with firearms. Ignorant of their proper use he becomes careless with them. He fails to realize that the firearm is a deadly weapon, not a toy. Accidents can happen to the expert, too, but usually he has learned that he can never be too careful. He knows that safety and care really add to the enjoyment of his sport.

It takes but a little good sense to handle a gun with caution and discrimination, and it pays. When a hunter uses his hunting equipment safely he promotes the success of his woodland ventures and assures himself fine hunting, adds color to his life, and returns refreshed from the workaday world.

In the handling of firearms, then, a few warnings might be considered. The one that is first and foremost is this: *always handle a gun as though it were loaded,* for it might be. There is no need to be afraid of your gun; just handle it with care and respect its capabilities. It is always a potentially dangerous weapon.

Some accidents are common, yet very much preventable. General among these is the one that happens when removing a gun from the car. Nothing would happen if the gun were not loaded, but it seems that some hunters like to carry loaded guns in their cars ready for a shot. Fortunately, some states have a law which prohibits carrying a loaded firearm in the car. This is not only a deterrent to illegal shooting from a vehicle, but certainly a wise and preventive measure against gun accidents of this sort. Check your gun; keep it empty when in the car; it is just that simple.

Check your gun from time to time, too, to make sure it is clean when hunting. It might become obstructed with mud, snow, water, or ice, in the course of the hunting day, and explode when the gun is fired. Do this by looking through the breech, not the muzzle. Make sure, too, that your gun and accessories are in first-class shape before starting the hunt. This takes but little time, and is certainly good hunting and shooting insurance.

The faulty gun is really a bad offender and something which can be avoided. Before season any man using a gun should make sure it is in safe and workable condition, and in good repair. The trigger pull is very important—a hair-trigger adjustment should be eliminated. If there is any doubt at all about the trigger action the firearm should be taken to a gunsmith for inspection and possible adjustment. The gun as a whole should be checked from time to time. Most modern guns are safe and strong, but a defect can develop.

The prospective hunter should learn how his gun works and why. Hunting accidents are usually the result of ignorance and carelessness, both with the gun itself and its handling. Many states have laws compelling young hunters to take and pass a safe-hunting course. Students who learn these lessons well become top-notch and conscientious hunters and shooters. Game wardens and volunteer instructors of the National Rifle Association give special classes for the beginning hunter, as well as the interested adult, and are doing a great service to the sport. In these courses the show-off, the undisciplined, the delinquent, is shown up for what he is and soon weeded out.

Some hunters fail to realize that the muzzle of a gun should never be pointed at anyone—at any time—including themselves. Take the case of the man who will draw a gun toward himself by the muzzle from a car or a stone wall or over a fence. This is a case of sheer stupidity, but accidents happen this way every year.

At no time should a gun be picked up but by the grip. Held in this position the muzzle naturally points in the other direction, usually toward the ground. By the way, if the muzzle is always pointed in that direction there is little danger shooting oneself or one's partner, providing the partner is not too close. I have seen pictures of hunters, adults at that, who seem to enjoy having their pictures taken while leaning on the muzzles of their guns. This is an off-beat stunt if there ever was one and should be discouraged as beginners might decide to try it.

A gun left unattended, while loaded, is highly explosive. Never should a loaded gun be left standing carelessly against a wall, a gun rack, or the bumper of a car.

It may fall over or be picked up by someone who knows little about guns, even if such a person has no business examining strange guns.

The loaded gun is really lethal when it is not unloaded before entering the house, camp, or automobile. In these places, especially, there is the temptation for some member of the party to pick up the gun, look it over, and try the mechanism, "to see how it works." Be sure your gun is unloaded when it is out of your hands, and keep it loaded only when in the field and actually hunting. Also, the practice of keeping only the unloaded gun in the house or camp should discourage anyone from picking up the gun and playfully aiming it at someone in the party. Should he pull the trigger no harm would result.

One thing some hunters find hard to learn is target identification. Something moves, or is even stationary, which looks like game, and they shoot. This, really, is criminal negligence; but it happens. Such was the case when a jittery hunter shot a man mistaken for a bear in the very early dawn on the opening day of the northern deer season. Some hunters shoot at a movement in the brush, or a sound, even when hunting small game. Imagining something that might be a game target in the cover, they shoot first and investigate later. Accidents can have serious repercussions on more than the victim, for the man who shoots another may experience a world of misery to his dying day.

Curiosity about a loaded firearm is another cause of accidents. If one must handle and inspect a gun, even his own, he had better make dead-sure first that the shells are out. Always point the gun at the ground at the same time. A companion of mine was inspecting the safety on my new shotgun and tried the trigger. The gun went off. But it fired harmlessly into the ground. I'm sure he learned a lesson from that. And so did I.

If there is any possibility that your shot at game will come too near your partner, by all means pass it up. When a party of men are hunting together great care must be exercised so that no one is injured. It is far better to pass up a shot than shoot anywhere near another hunter. When traveling on a trail it is best that no more than two hunters walk abreast, one on each side of the road, and let the man take the shot on whose side of the road the game appears.

Another bad practice is to carry two gauges of shells in the hunting jacket. The 16-gauge will not drop through the 12-bore, but a 20-gauge will, sliding down until the rim strikes the cone. If a 12-gauge is placed on top of it and the gun fired, the 20-bore shell will explode right where the barrel is thinnest with disastrous effect. It will ruin the gun and may cause serious injury to the hand. Watch out, too, for high-power shells in an old gun with thin barrels! Some shotguns were made to handle field loads exclusively and not the Magnum shells.

The "empty" gun, especially in the home, is a triple-threat offender. Supposedly unloaded, someone picks it up, perhaps playfully, aims it at someone, and pulls the trigger. To prevent this accident all cartridges should be removed from the gun as soon as the hunter is through hunting and replaced only at the start of another hunt.

Never should a gun be regarded as empty unless one is very certain of it. At home the safest place for a gun is in a gun cabinet, unloaded and locked, so that no one, either young or old, can handle it.

Since gun accidents cannot be prevented by any legal means short of barring the use of them altogether, the whole thing is simply a matter of common sense and consideration for others. The man who is careful with firearms will derive most from them as well as have more hunting companions. A man who is careless with guns will soon be shunned by other sportsmen, even his own friends, if he fails to conform. I have met such individuals who just will not learn. It pays in countless ways to be a safe hunter in order to keep hunting the wonderful sport it is.

It is wonderful and it is popular. One out of every ten American males over fifteen owns a shotgun or rifle; there are 15 million hunting licenses issued annually.

The sport of hunting, especially deer hunting, is growing. Be a careful hunter. Stress safety. Show your companions by your actions how a gun should be handled and cared for. Go hunting as much as you can. Go bird hunting, rabbit hunting, duck hunting, and then climax the season with a go after the best of them all, the whitetail buck. Store up memories you'll never forget.